LET THE PEOPLE HEAR IT

CONCERTS FROM THE LIBRARY OF CONGRESS AT 100

LET THE PEOPLE HEAR IT

CONCERTS FROM THE LIBRARY OF CONGRESS AT 100

by Nicholas A. Brown-Cáceres and David H. Plylar

Washington, DC

ISBN 978-0-8444-9594-1 (softcover)
ISBN 978-0-8444-9596-5 (hardcover)

Library of Congress Cataloging-in-Publication Data

Names: Cáceres-Brown, Nicholas A. author | Plylar, David author | Vita, Susan H. | Harrington, David (Violinist)

Title: Let the people hear it : Concerts from the Library of Congress at 100 / by Nicholas A. Cáceres-Brown and David H. Plylar.

Description: [First.]. | Washington, DC : Library of Congress, 2025. | Series: Collection close-ups ; book 3 | Includes bibliographical references and index. | Summary: "The Concerts from the Library of Congress series, presented by the Library's Music Division, has been one of the Library's flagship public engagement initiatives since its founding in 1925. The series was made possible through the groundbreaking philanthropic contributions of Elizabeth Sprague Coolidge, who was committed to making the Library of Congress a premiere international presenter of live music of the highest caliber, free to the public. This vision was realized through building the historic Coolidge Auditorium, establishing an endowment to support concerts, and creating the Library's music commissioning program that has contributed 650+ new works to the repertoire in classical music and jazz. This book celebrates the centennial of this internationally important concert series and brings the Library's music and performing arts collections to life through captivating images and engaging text"-- Provided by publisher.

Identifiers: LCCN 2025026759 | ISBN 9780844495941 paperback | ISBN 9780844495965 hardcover

Subjects: LCSH: Coolidge Auditorium (Library of Congress)--History | Concerts from the Library of Congress--History | Concerts--Washington (D.C.)--History | Coolidge, Elizabeth Sprague, 1864-1953

Classification: LCC ML38.W2 C664 2025 | DDC 780.78/753--dc23/eng/20250819
LC record available at https://lccn.loc.gov/2025026759

Designed by Cindy Moore Weigel

Printed in Canada

This book is dedicated to the memory of Susan H. Vita, Chief of the Music Division from 2005-2025.

During her tenure, Vita oversaw a fifth of the concert series' history, expanding its scope, reach, and footprint while maintaining its reputation as a cultural beacon. A tireless public servant, she served through the conclusion of the 100th season, a milestone of which the American people can be proud. The authors are profoundly indebted to her for her support and vision, which laid the groundwork for the next hundred years of Concerts from the Library of Congress.

Contents

The Dalí Quartet and clarinetist Ricardo Morales performed the Stradivari Anniversary Concert on December 18, 2023, in the Coolidge Auditorium, Thomas Jefferson Building. The quartet played on the Library's historic Stradivari instruments.

Foreword

Since 1925, the Library of Congress has been a premiere destination for experiencing live music and the performing arts in the nation's capital. Our treasured concert series, Concerts from the Library of Congress, was founded through a groundbreaking public-private partnership with philanthropist Elizabeth Sprague Coolidge, and it continues to serve as a key access point for Americans to connect with their national library. The experience of hearing music written as recently as the current year and as far back as the Middle Ages provides music lovers an unparalleled opportunity to witness new interpretations of creative works that the Library preserves in its collections.

The storied concert series—which has commissioned masterworks such as the Pulitzer Prize–winning classic *Appalachian Spring* by Aaron Copland with choreography by Martha Graham and Béla Bartók's Fifth String Quartet—serves audiences in Washington, DC, as well as across the country and internationally through radio broadcasts, virtual concerts, and commercial recordings. Over the years, audiences have been treated to special appearances by artists across genres and performing traditions, ranging from the Hampton Institute Choir and Juilliard String Quartet to Broadway sensation Audra McDonald and Pulitzer Prize–winning composer and conductor John Adams. The Library's commitment to access and the vision established by Coolidge ensures that performances by these iconic artists are available free of charge to the public. "Let the People Hear It," the title of this book, comes from a tribute from President Franklin D. Roosevelt and other civic leaders to Coolidge on her eightieth birthday in 1944 and reflects the philosophy of open access to the performing arts that the Library of Congress holds dear. I am grateful to the generations of supporters, including former Speaker of the House Nicholas Longworth and the Friends of Music, who have contributed to sustaining this access.

Throughout this book, readers will discover many of the people and memorable stories that compose the history of our concert series through photographs, music manuscripts, and rare documents from the Library's Music Division and Prints and Photographs Division. In celebrating the centennial of Concerts from the Library of Congress, I invite you to explore how America's oldest federal cultural institution contributes to artistic creativity and innovation rooted in the vibrant, diverse musical and performing arts heritage that nourishes our communities. In addition to discovering the history of the series through this book, you can watch hundreds of videos of performances and explore related collections at loc.gov.

Susan H. Vita
Chief, Music Division, Library of Congress (2005–2025)

Grammy Award–winning singer-songwriter Gregory Porter receives applause during his March 8, 2014, concert in the Coolidge Auditorium.

Preface

Few occasions in the history of the Library of Congress have been as consequential to the evolution of the nation's first federal cultural institution as the founding of the Concerts from the Library of Congress series in 1925. Over the course of a century, the Library's concert series and the initial vision of philanthropist Elizabeth Sprague Coolidge have inspired the Library of Congress's efforts to engage researchers, philanthropists, creators, and the public. With the help of Carl Engel, who served as chief of the Music Division from 1922 to 1934, and Herbert Putnam, the eighth Librarian of Congress, Coolidge enshrined in an act of Congress the central role of music in the identity of the United States. Her initiative to share music and the Library's work through the performing arts continues to make an indelible mark on the fabric of our cultural heritage.

Coolidge's pioneering goal—to make chamber music accessible to all Americans, through free performances by leading artists, commissioning new music, and radio broadcasts—was decades ahead of its time for its exploration of repertoire both old and new. Her commitment to investing in artists and expanding the Library of Congress's reach distinguished a bespoke model of philanthropic giving that has been embraced by countless benefactors since the 1920s, from Gertrude Clarke Whittall, who donated a quintet of Stradivari instruments and dozens of priceless music manuscripts, to the many Friends of Music contributors, who share a zeal for continuing Coolidge's work. Her legacy continues to inspire the Library's embrace of innovative ways to connect community members with its collections, whether through digital engagement, television broadcasts, educational resources, or memorable visits to the Library's campus on Capitol Hill.

> ***"The Library's concerts have won Washington an international reputation as one of the world's great chamber music centers. It would be difficult to find a renowned ensemble which has not, at one time or another, performed in the Coolidge Auditorium."***
>
> —Irving Lowens, *Evening Star,* Washington, DC, May 26, 1963

Thousands of events have taken place during the illustrious history of Concerts from the Library of Congress. While this volume cannot claim to be comprehensive, it gives a taste of the extraordinarily rich history of great performances and significant commissions performed at the Library over one hundred years. As the Library marks this special anniversary, the stories of the people and creative expression that have found a home in the Coolidge Auditorium—the Library's primary performance venue—will continue to enrich America's performing arts scene in unexpected and unmissable ways.

Anne E. McLean and Michele L. Glymph
Senior Producers for Concerts and Special Projects
Music Division

Overture

David Harrington views manuscripts from the Music Division's collections on the occasion of Kronos Quartet's fiftieth anniversary concert at the Library, April 4, 2024.

The Coolidge Auditorium at the Library of Congress in Washington, DC, is a mythic, iconic place for music and musicians. A concert venue only becomes legendary when inspiring musical events take place there over a long period of time. My first encounter with the Coolidge Auditorium was through a gift my teacher Veda Reynolds gave me in 1975 when the Kronos Quartet was about to leave Seattle: the amazing live recording of Joseph Szigeti and Béla Bartók performing in 1940 and released as a double LP on Vanguard.

There is an urgency and completeness combined with a beautiful freshness in every note they played on April 13, 1940, at the Coolidge Auditorium. Bartók had arrived in the United States just two days earlier, after a long boat journey from Europe. He then had to get from New York City to Washington, DC, in time for the concert. Wasn't he completely exhausted? When did he and Szigeti rehearse? World War II was spreading like a horrible infection. There was alarm and huge concern for the future of freedom. As I first listened to this recording, I was gripped and challenged by the strength and expressive power of these incredible visionary artists from their first notes of Beethoven's "Kreutzer" sonata. All the way through the entire concert it was clear this performance was a journey, a vital examination of culture and expression unique in recorded history. When I listened again to this record recently, Veda's teaching still informs me after all these years, and Szigeti and Bartók's performance continues to provide a beacon for a way forward I find very useful right now.

When I learned in 2023 that Kronos was to have our fiftieth-year concert at the Library of Congress on April 18, 2024, I knew we had to create a panoramic musical experience that deserved to be on the Coolidge Auditorium stage. In addition to the Szigeti/Bartók concert, I also learned that the Library commissioned and presented the premiere of *Appalachian Spring* by Martha Graham and Aaron Copland (1944). Odetta, one of the essential voices of our Civil Rights era, had performed on that stage, and the premiere of George Crumb's startling *Ancient Voices of Children* (1970) happened there, as did the amazing 1938 recording sessions when Alan Lomax interviewed Jelly Roll Morton about his life and the early days of jazz. Many other wondrous musical moments have happened at Coolidge Auditorium, resulting in a historical resonance one can feel there that demands the very best from musicians. I wanted Kronos to make a concert unlike any we had ever played. So I started gathering together music that might be able to tell something of our country's history, a few of its stories, and demonstrate even a bit of what exists for all of us to explore at the American Folklife Center in the Library of Congress.

This curation process took many months and finally resulted in a program ranging from Scott Johnson's *How it Happens: The Voice of I. F. Stone* (honoring Stone, a DC native and one of America's most gifted, exuberant, and incisive investigative reporters) and Gullah church music (*Testimony* by Charlton Singleton), to *Peace Be Till* by Zachary Watkins (which tells the story of how MLK's "I Have a Dream" speech became the speech we all know) and Jimi Hendrix's "Purple Haze," among other powerful pieces.

Szigeti and Bartók set the bar so incredibly high for live artistic expression. All anyone else can do is their very best. The fabled musical air in Coolidge Auditorium gave me and all of Kronos a challenge we tried to meet with every fiber of our beings. This challenge was the result of nearly one hundred years of performances that have helped shape the musical life in our country.

Congratulations to the Library of Congress on one hundred years of concerts and commissions. Let's make it two hundred years!

David Harrington
Founder, Artistic Director, and Violinist, Kronos Quartet
2024 Kluge Chair in Modern Culture

Portrait of Elizabeth and Albert Sprague Coolidge by Julius Garibaldi (Gari) Melchers (1860–1932), 1902. This portrait is on display in the lobby of the Coolidge Auditorium. Elizabeth and her son Sprague, as he was known, both had opportunities to perform on their namesake stage. Coolidge appeared as a pianist on December 2, 1927, and December 20, 1928. Sprague appeared as a violist in a performance of Vincent d'Indy's op. 92 string quartet for the Founder's Day concert—honoring his mother's birthday—in 1932. He played oboe in the Founder's Day concert of 1951 with the Kroll Quartet that featured works composed by his mother.

Prologue

Mrs. Coolidge Goes to Washington

On an autumn evening in 1925, the joyful, buoyant sounds of a Bach chorale prelude for solo organ first rang out from the new music venue at the Library of Congress, an occasion that marked a thrilling new endeavor. The 485-seat auditorium was the brainchild of philanthropist and musician Elizabeth Sprague Coolidge (1864-1953) and Carl Engel (1883-1944), chief of the Library of Congress Music Division.

The inaugural Library of Congress Festival of Chamber Music launched the next chapter of Coolidge's creative enterprise, which involved promoting chamber music and living composers to audiences throughout the United States and Europe. By an act of Congress, the Library of Congress was now the permanent home for Coolidge's chamber music concerts, which she required would always remain "freely open to the national public as any other exhibits in the Library of Congress." Her bold vision to make chamber music accessible to the widest possible audience was backed by her philanthropic commitment and a belief that the United States government should have an active role in advancing the musical arts.

Setting the Stage

Coolidge and Engel had worked for more than two years to revolutionize the scope of the Library of Congress's musical activities. With assistance from Librarian of Congress Herbert Putnam (1861-1955), they secured bipartisan support in Congress to establish a legal mechanism for the Library to accept private funds to build the concert hall and establish a trust fund for presenting concerts and commissioning new music—and Congress passed the necessary laws only five months after Coolidge's first letter of intent. This would be a staggering feat today, but it is even more impressive during an era when correspondence was handled via the postal service and telegram. Coolidge was also traveling around the United States presenting concerts, her lawyer was in Boston, her funds were managed in Chicago, and Engel and Putnam were in Washington working through committees in both the House of Representatives and the Senate.

Just ten months after the legislation was signed into law, an audience

Carl Engel , pictured here in 1922, served as chief of the Library's Music Division from 1922 to 1934.

that included First Lady Grace Anna Coolidge (no relation to Elizabeth Sprague Coolidge), government leaders, diplomats, leading musicians, and music lovers gathered for an eclectic array of performances in late October 1925. The Library of Congress quickly developed a global reputation for presenting chamber music with a strong commitment to both standard repertoire and new music. Composers and international touring ensembles took notice of the support Coolidge was offering for living composers and musical acts that championed new music, in particular. Coolidge had cemented her legacy and forever entwined chamber music with the identity of the Library of Congress.

Mrs. C: Becoming the Fairy Godmother of Music

Elizabeth's background as a pianist and composer, the personal challenges she faced as an adult, and her resilience prepared her to achieve her expansive vision for making chamber music more accessible to the American people. Born in Chicago in 1864 to Albert Arnold Sprague and Nancy Ann Atwood Sprague, Elizabeth was exposed to music, philanthropy, and entrepreneurship from her youth. Her father was a graduate of Yale University and a successful businessman in the wholesale grocery industry. Albert served on cultural institution boards, including for the Chicago Symphony Orchestra. Her mother was an amateur musician and supported Elizabeth's study of piano and composition. Elizabeth attended an elite dual language (French/English) boarding school in New York, traveled extensively in Europe, and eventually married Harvard-educated orthopedic surgeon Frederic Shurtleff Coolidge of Boston in 1891. Elizabeth and Frederic had one son, Albert Sprague Coolidge, in 1894, who studied violin, viola, and oboe in his youth.

Elizabeth spent her thirties and forties enjoying the bountiful cultural scene in Chicago until tragedy struck. Her father passed on January 10, 1915, followed by her husband four months later, on May 15, and her mother died the

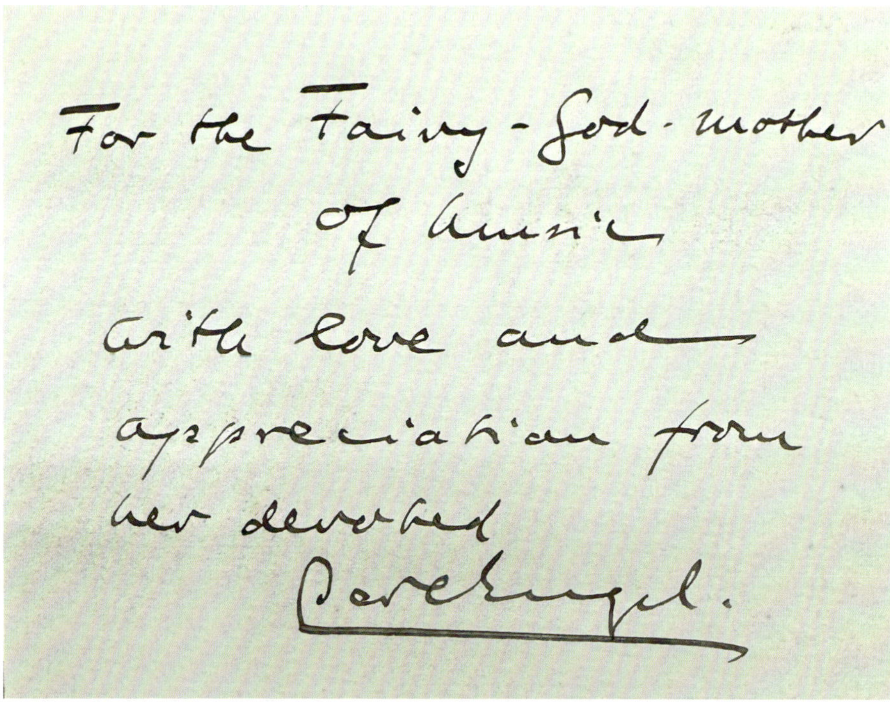
For the Fairy-God-mother
of music
with love and
appreciation from
her devoted
Carl Engel.

Left: Note from Engel to Coolidge, whom he endearingly referred to as the "Fairy-God-mother of music," ca. 1930s.

Right: Charcoal drawing of Elizabeth Sprague Coolidge by John Singer Sargent, 1923.

following March. Frederic's decline was particularly traumatizing. He accidentally contracted a bacterial infection from a patient during a surgical procedure in 1895, which led to numerous other afflictions, including tuberculosis and strokes. The family moved to rural New York and later the Berkshires to care for Frederic until his death.

Throughout this period, Elizabeth's financial responsibilities changed dramatically. She inherited almost $2 million from her father's estate and another $2 million from her mother's, while assuming the role of head of household following her husband's death. After her father's death, she made her first major philanthropic contribution, a gift of $100,000 to the Chicago Symphony to establish the orchestra's pension fund, a first for American symphony orchestras. The gift began Coolidge's thirty-eight-year career as a major philanthropist. In addition to her music philanthropy, she was active in medical causes. She donated two properties in Chicago to provide lodging for nurses, established a trust fund for a specialized hospital, funded medical research fellowships at Columbia University, and contributed money and her Berkshires property to the Berkshire County Society for Crippled Children.

The 1919 Berkshire Chamber Music Competition jury, photographed during the weekend of August 23–24, 1919. From left to right: Louis Bailly, Harold Bauer, Richard Aldrich, Frederick A. Stock, Coolidge, Hugo Kortschak, Georges Longy, and Rubin Goldmark. Coolidge's reputation as a leading music philanthropist grew as her Berkshire Festival drew influential artists, industry leaders, and audiences.

Though she was active as a pianist and frequent concertgoer, Coolidge further immersed herself in music as a coping mechanism for her losses. She processed her emotions through intense piano practice, gave private lessons, and continued to compose, though she would later describe her efforts as decidedly "amateur." In the period after her husband died but before her mother passed, Coolidge's financial support for musical institutions expanded significantly. With her mother, she funded the building of Sprague Memorial Hall at Yale (1917), in honor of her alumnus father. This was the first of four concert halls she eventually had a hand in building, along with the South Mountain Concert Hall (Pittsfield, Massachusetts; 1918), the Coolidge Auditorium (Library of Congress, Washington, DC; 1925), and the concert hall at Mills College (Oakland, California; 1928).

In the late 1910s and early 1920s, Coolidge's profile as a patron of the arts blossomed. She established the Berkshire Quartet (1916), the Berkshire Festival (1918), and a Berkshire Chamber Music Competition for composition (1918), and she began to fund performances of distinguished ensembles such as the Pro Arte Quartet.

Finding a Permanent Home

Rather than providing a permanent gift, Coolidge preferred to provide "seed money" for concerts in the hope that once being exposed to the delights of chamber music, local enthusiasts would continue to support the concerts. Coolidge also believed in creating platforms for contemporary music. This motivated her to commission living composers, primarily Americans and Europeans, and to underwrite performances of their pieces along with standard repertoire that would entice audiences.

After Coolidge and Music Division Chief Engel met at the Berkshire Festival in September 1922, he encouraged her to donate the manuscripts of her commissioned

> ***My plea for modern music is not that we should like it, nor necessarily that we should even understand it, but that we should exhibit it as a significant human document."***
>
> - Elizabeth Sprague Coolidge, Address to the National Federation of Music Clubs, ca. 1940s.

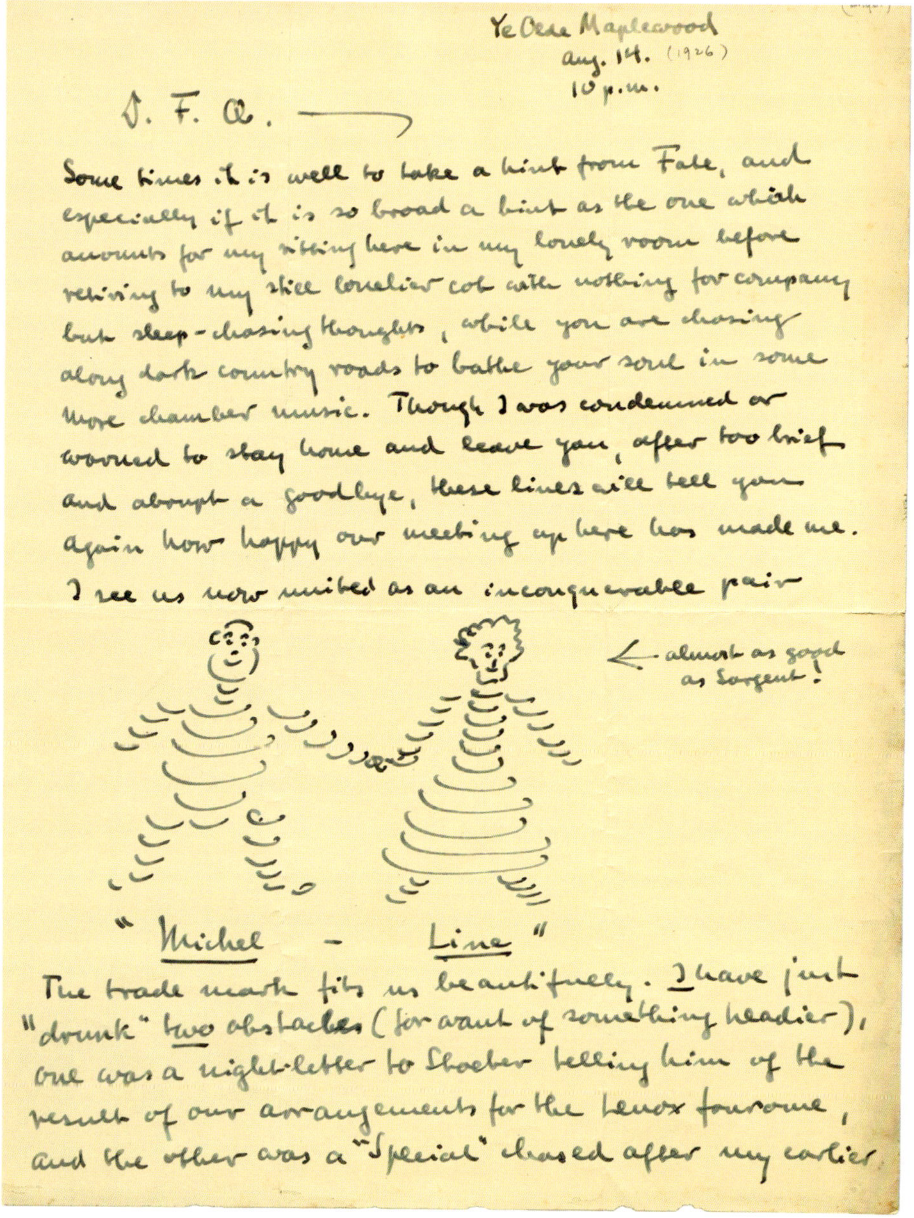

Ye Olde Maplewood
Aug. 14. (1926)
10 p.m.

E. S. C. ⟶

Some times it is well to take a hint from Fate, and especially if it is so broad a hint as the one which accounts for my sitting here in my lonely room before retiring to my still lonelier cot with nothing for company but sleep-chasing thoughts, while you are chasing along dark country roads to bathe your soul in some more chamber music. Though I was condemned or warned to stay home and leave you, after too brief and abrupt a goodbye, these lines will tell you again how happy our meeting up here has made me. I see us now united as an inconquerable pair

← almost as good as Sargent!

"Michel - Line"

The trade mark fits us beautifully. I have just "drunk" two obstacles (for want of something headier), one was a night-letter to Stoeber telling him of the result of our arrangements for the Lenox foursome, and the other was a "Special" chased after my earlier

Engel created nicknames for himself and Coolidge based on the contemporaneous Michelin tire slogan *Le pneu Michelin boit l'obstacle* ("The Michelin tire overcomes the obstacle"), an homage to their uncanny ability to navigate the federal bureaucracy. Engel drew sketches of them in the form of the Michelin Man, and noted the drawing is "almost as good as Sargent!," referring to John Singer Sargent's charcoal portrait of Coolidge from 1923.

works to the Library for its collections. On October 5, 1922, Engel revisited his proposal, writing to Coolidge that "It would seem but fitting that your fine collection be some day placed with our [n]ational library, as a permanent testimony to the ideals and munificence of a remarkable American woman." By 1923, Coolidge began transferring her music manuscript collection to the Library's Music Division, and she and Engel began to conceive of concerts in Washington, DC, although Librarian Putnam was hesitant to expand the operational scope of the Library—because, as Engel relayed in November 1923, "there is no suitable auditorium in the Library building."

Engel and Coolidge were undeterred. Engel had long desired to host concerts at the Library to enhance the relevance of the Music Division's collections and share them with a wider audience. He and Coolidge approached the Smithsonian Institution's Freer Gallery of Art, which had a newly-constructed auditorium, while also developing a plan to create a "suitable" venue at the Library. "How proud I am that your Library, my Library, and my Government, is willing to do all this for the Festival [of] Music!" Coolidge wrote to Putnam on December 26, 1923, after receiving indication that the Library would move forward with presenting concerts at an alternate venue.

Left: Message to invited guests of the Library of Congress-Coolidge concerts held at the Freer Auditorium in February 1924. The death of former president Woodrow Wilson on February 3 caused organizers to question if it would be appropriate to hold the concerts as scheduled, but the concerts went on as planned.

Right: Program booklet from the Library of Congress-Coolidge concerts at the Freer auditorium in February 1924.

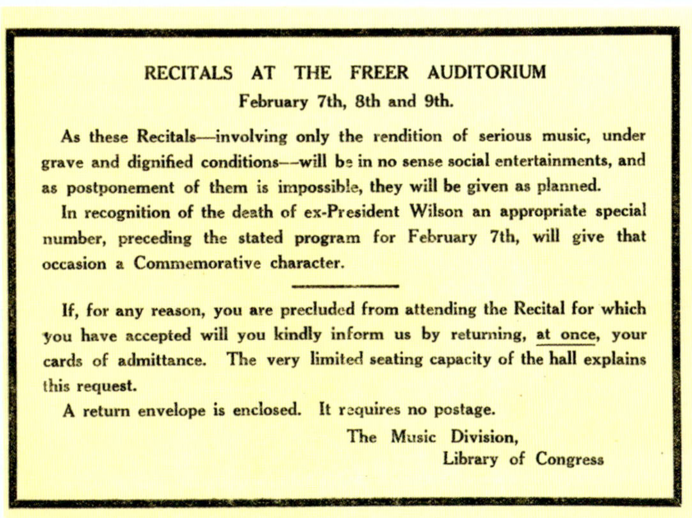

RECITALS AT THE FREER AUDITORIUM
February 7th, 8th and 9th.

As these Recitals—involving only the rendition of serious music, under grave and dignified conditions—will be in no sense social entertainments, and as postponement of them is impossible, they will be given as planned.

In recognition of the death of ex-President Wilson an appropriate special number, preceding the stated program for February 7th, will give that occasion a Commemorative character.

If, for any reason, you are precluded from attending the Recital for which you have accepted will you kindly inform us by returning, at once, your cards of admittance. The very limited seating capacity of the hall explains this request.

A return envelope is enclosed. It requires no postage.

The Music Division,
Library of Congress

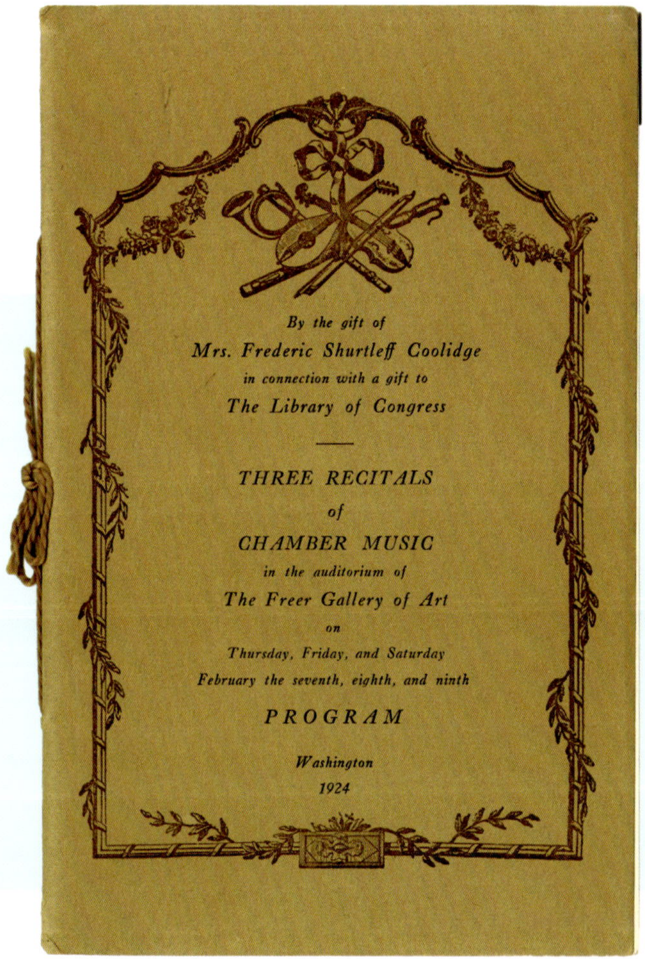

On February 7, 8, and 9, 1924, Coolidge and Engel presented the first Library of Congress-Coolidge Festival of Chamber Music, "by the courtesy of the authorities of the Smithsonian Institution," at the Freer Gallery of Art auditorium. Featured were the Berkshire Quartet, the Elshuco Trio, and the Lenox Quartet, with guests, in programs that mixed standard and contemporary repertoire. The invitation list for these concerts included senior government and diplomatic officials, major figures in the Washington music community, and musicians associated with Coolidge from as far away as Boston, such as composer and violist Rebecca Clarke. The response to these concerts was overwhelmingly positive.

Following the concerts at the Freer Gallery, Coolidge mobilized her legal and financial advisors to begin negotiations with Putnam and Engel for building a new auditorium

Letter dated January 25, 1924, from Laura Harlan, White House social secretary, to Librarian of Congress Herbert Putnam, accepting on behalf of First Lady Grace Coolidge the Library's invitation to attend the February 8 concert at the Freer auditorium. While Elizabeth Sprague Coolidge was not related to President Calvin Coolidge and the First Lady, correspondence intended for her occasionally was sent to the White House and vice versa.

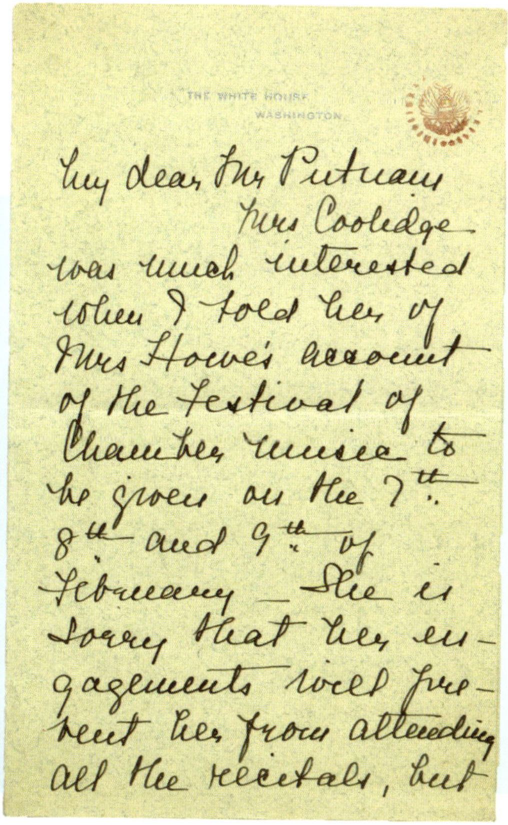
THE WHITE HOUSE
WASHINGTON

My dear Mr Putnam
Mrs Coolidge was much interested when I told her of Mrs Howe's account of the Festival of Chamber music to be given on the 7th, 8th and 9th of February — She is sorry that her engagements will prevent her from attending all the recitals, but

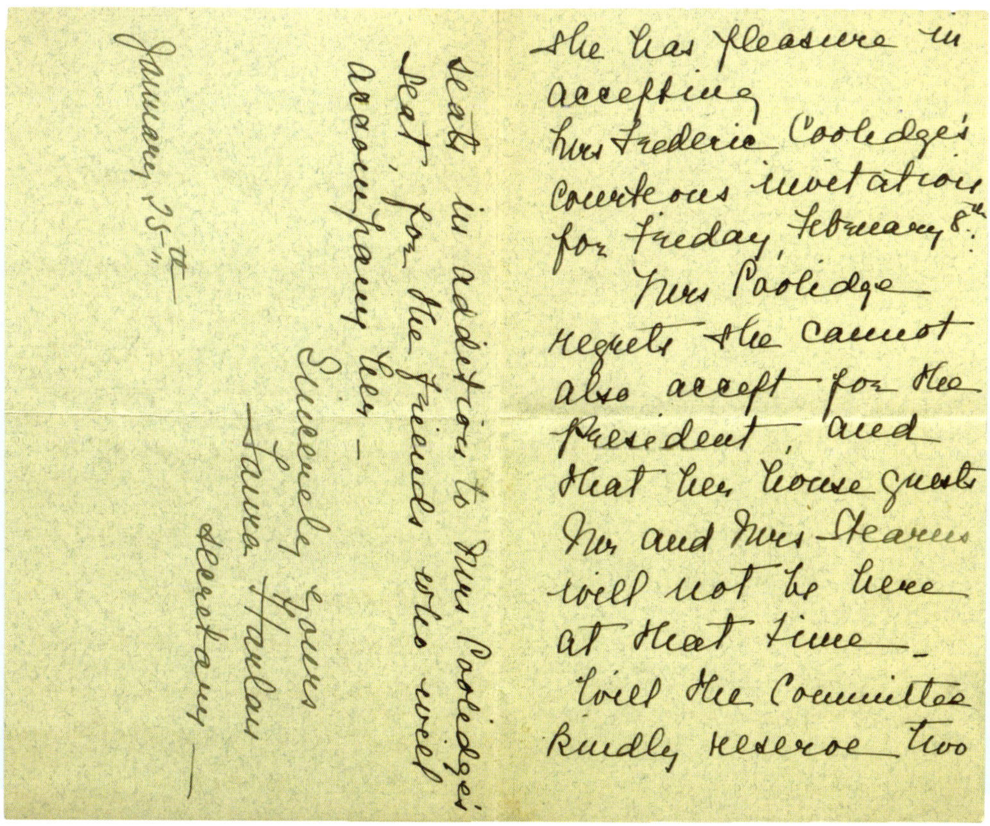
she has pleasure in accepting Mrs Frederic Coolidge's courteous invitation for Friday, February 8th. Mrs Coolidge regrets she cannot also accept for the President, and that her house guests Mr and Mrs Stearns will not be here at that time — Will the Committee kindly reserve two seats in addition to Mrs Coolidge's seat, for the friends who will accompany her —

Sincerely Yours
Laura Harlan
Secretary —

January 25th

at the Library. The extensive correspondence from these months between Coolidge, her principal attorney Richard W. Hale, Engel, and Putnam reveals her to be a shrewd businesswoman with effective advisors. Hale recommended modelling Coolidge's gift agreement after James Smithson's donation of the Smithsonian Institution to the federal government, but as a legislative agency, the Library would require an act of Congress to administer and accept Coolidge's gift.

Once legislation was drafted and introduced in Congress, the next steps quickly fell into place. Coolidge's formal offer committed $112,500 to fund the construction of a concert hall with pristine acoustics for chamber music. She also committed to establishing an endowment for concerts with an initial contribution of $123,438.20 in securities. Additional larger gifts arrived in the 1950s, both while Coolidge was alive and through her estate.

> ***"I wanted you to know how much Mrs. Pepper and I appreciated the music of Mrs. Frederick Coolidge. We hope we may have the pleasure of hearing her again."***
>
> —Senator George W. Pepper in a letter to Librarian Putnam, February 16, 1924

Within a week of her offer, on December 10, 1924, Senator George W. Pepper of Pennsylvania introduced legislation to accept Coolidge's gift in the US Senate, and it passed five days later. Representative Robert Luce of Massachusetts sponsored the House version, which passed on January 19, 1925. President Calvin Coolidge signed the legislation four days later. A second bill creating the Library of Congress Trust Fund Board to accept and administer Coolidge's trust similarly passed through Congress in a matter of weeks, with President Coolidge signing it into law on March 3. There was no time to lose: Elizabeth Sprague Coolidge and Engel planned to open the hall just nine months later for a festival of chamber music on Coolidge's birthday weekend.

Coolidge moved the federal government in a way few have managed, but her staying power

Coolidge was so eager for her vision to be realized that she delivered a check for $60,000 (c/o Herbert Putnam) to Engel in November 1924, two months before the Library could legally accept her funds.

is revealed in the purpose of her efforts, as she expressed to Putnam in 1926:

> *If the Elizabeth Sprague Coolidge Foundation might foster the interests of musicians, both creative and interpretative, by freeing them from the power of advertising middlemen such as manufacturers, managers, publishers and critics, I should consider it a service, rendered by a small corner of our Government, to Art, to America, and therefore to the idealism of the world.*

Coolidge desired to invite others into the world of music that had saved her during her darkest hours. She believed in the good that government could do in nurturing the arts, and her vision was larger than just building concert halls and presenting free concerts. She wanted the arts to be central to American civic identity.

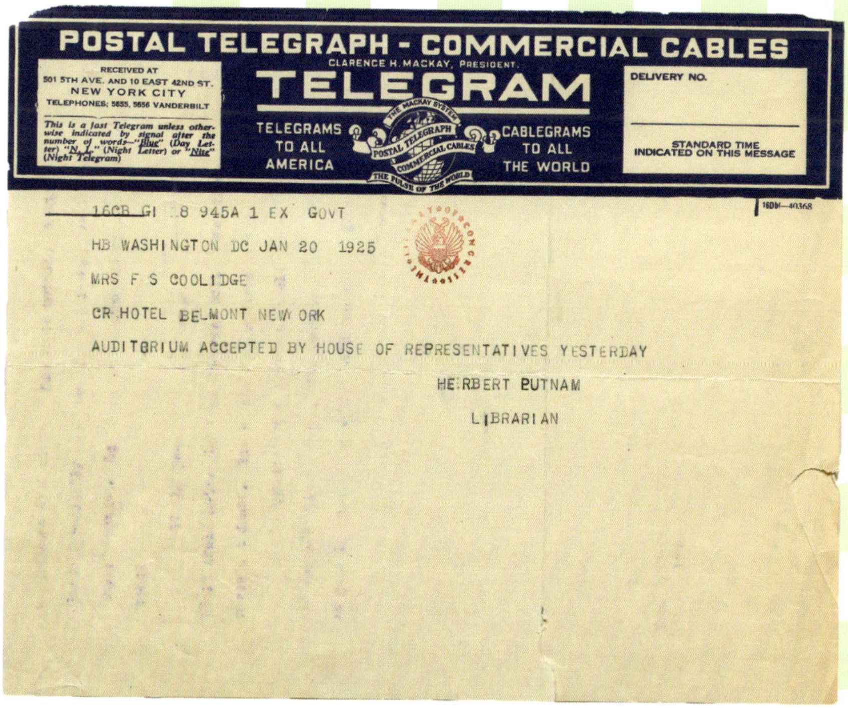

POSTAL TELEGRAPH - COMMERCIAL CABLES

CLARENCE H. MACKAY, PRESIDENT.

TELEGRAM

RECEIVED AT 501 5TH AVE. AND 10 EAST 42ND ST. NEW YORK CITY TELEPHONES: 5655, 5656 VANDERBILT

This is a fast Telegram unless otherwise indicated by signal after the number of words—"Blue" (Day Letter) "N L" (Night Letter) or "Nite" (Night Telegram)

TELEGRAMS TO ALL AMERICA

CABLEGRAMS TO ALL THE WORLD

DELIVERY NO.

STANDARD TIME INDICATED ON THIS MESSAGE

16CB GI 8 945A 1 EX GOVT

HB WASHINGTON DC JAN 20 1925

MRS F S COOLIDGE

CR HOTEL BELMONT NEW ORK

AUDITORIUM ACCEPTED BY HOUSE OF REPRESENTATIVES YESTERDAY

HERBERT PUTNAM

LIBRARIAN

Top: Workers begin construction on the Coolidge Auditorium within the Northwest Courtyard of the original Library of Congress building, later known as the Thomas Jefferson Building (1897), May 8, 1925.

Bottom: Telegram from Librarian of Congress Herbert Putnam to Coolidge notifying her that the legislation accepting the gift of the auditorium at the Library passed the House of Representatives, January 20, 1925.

Librarian of Congress Herbert Putnam in his office in the Thomas Jefferson Building, December 20, 1901.

Securing the Coolidge Legacy

After the inaugural Coolidge Festival, Coolidge remained involved in discussions about repertoire, artist selection, reception planning, and guest lists. She did not hesitate to express her opinions, such as her disdain for requiring patrons to pay a nominal service charge for their "free" tickets (processing fees were eliminated in 2015). Coolidge contributed additional funds on numerous occasions when investment returns fell short of projections, including during the Great Depression. When W. Oliver Strunk (1901-1980) succeeded Engel as chief of the Music Division in 1934, Coolidge was quick to notify Herbert Putnam of her displeasure with Strunk's speed of correspondence and management of her trust fund. She was involved in planning concerts until her death in 1953, though her level of engagement fluctuated as her health declined.

Coolidge's influence continues as the Library's concert series and commissioning program enters its second century. More than seven hundred works have been commissioned by the Library, inclusive of the Coolidge Foundation commissions, Koussevitzky Music Foundation commissions, and works commissioned by other gift and trust funds. Hundreds of thousands of visitors have witnessed memorable concerts by leading artists and have viewed associated music manuscripts and artifacts held by the Music Division.

Coolidge's vision to make concerts accessible to a national audience through radio broadcasts resulted in the series reaching listeners nationwide from the 1920s to the 1990s on a weekly basis, and again in the 2000s and 2010s through special broadcast series, bringing chamber music into the homes of everyday Americans.

Librarian Putnam's April 24, 1931, address to the Library of Congress Trust Fund Board best summarizes the immediate impact of Coolidge's 1925 gifts:

> *Six years ago a remarkable thing happened. A private citizen induced a government complacent in the efficiency of its operations to adopt an entirely new role, adopt it also as if to the manner born; persuaded a government concerned only with the "utilities" to accept as a utility something far more subtle than those of the grosser sort which alone it had deemed within its province. And then, having inspired the necessary convictions, she herself provided the resources for giving them practical effect. She did all this without organization, without the exercise of any political influence—did it single-handed. (This is her habit—except that when she gives, she gives with both hands.) The consequences of all this may be such as no man can foresee—and only one woman.*

TO

ELIZABETH SPRAGUE COOLIDGE

ON HER EIGHTIETH BIRTHDAY

OCTOBER 30, 1944

THE LIBRARY OF CONGRESS presents this volume to Elizabeth Sprague Coolidge *on her eightieth birthday as a token of gratitude and esteem. The Elizabeth Sprague Coolidge Foundation, which she established, has made the Library of Congress pre-eminent in chamber music. It has sponsored the creation of chamber music by some of the greatest of living composers. It has given chamber music to all parts of the Republic. It has served as a model for other foundations in other fields. For this enrichment of the services which the Library of Congress is able to render to the people of the United States, the Library is profoundly grateful.* Elizabeth Sprague Coolidge *has done what none before her had found the means to do—she has given the music on the shelves of the Library a living voice and let the people hear it.*

and let the people hear it.

This eightieth birthday tribute to Coolidge was signed by President Franklin Delano Roosevelt, Vice President Henry A. Wallace, Speaker of the House Sam Rayburn, ninth Librarian of Congress Archibald MacLeish, eighth Librarian of Congress Herbert Putnam, and tenth Librarian of Congress Luther H. Evans. The closing line, "let the people hear it," celebrates Coolidge's commitment to providing public access to the arts through the free concert series at the Library.

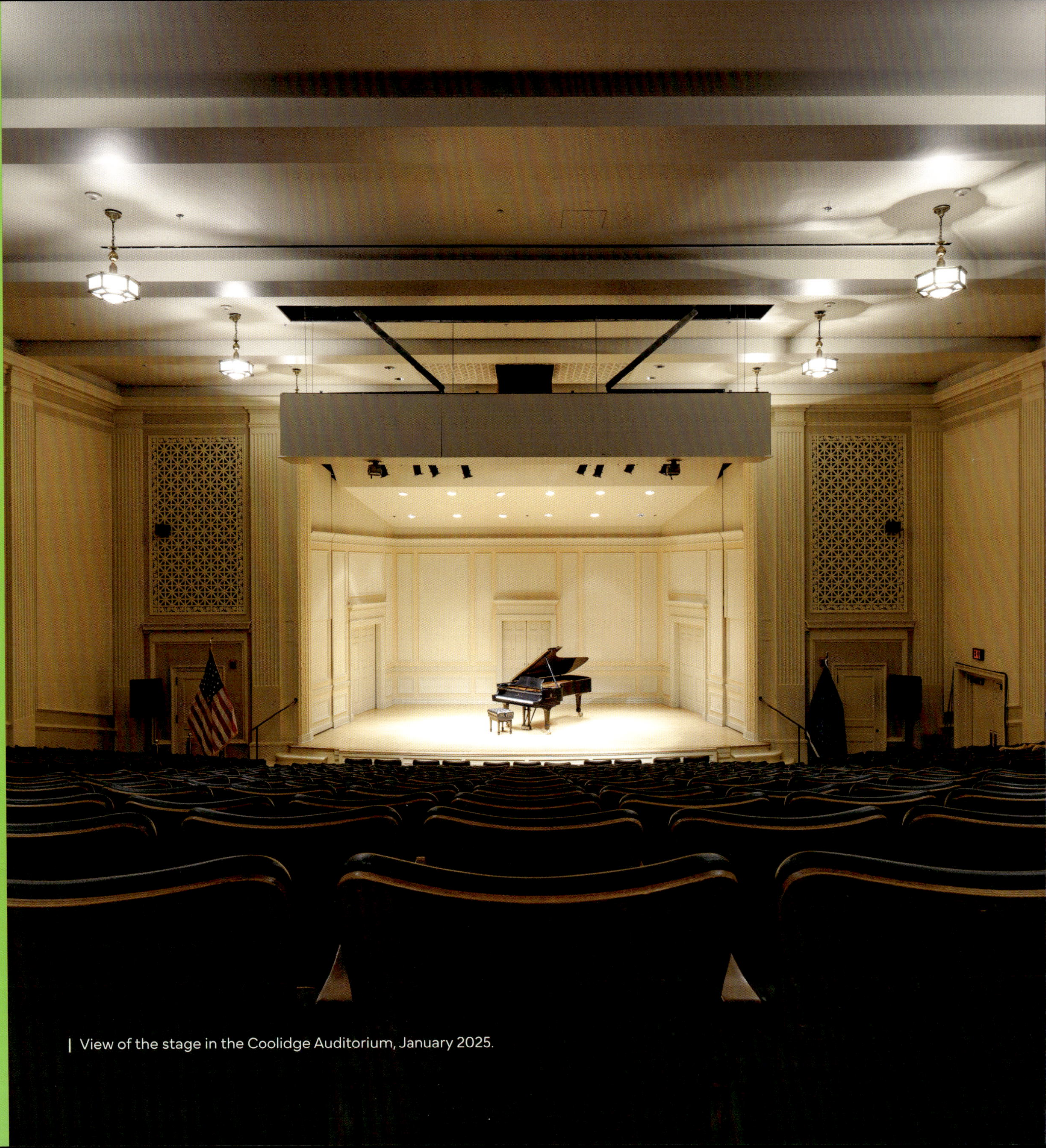

View of the stage in the Coolidge Auditorium, January 2025.

Act I

Performers and Composers

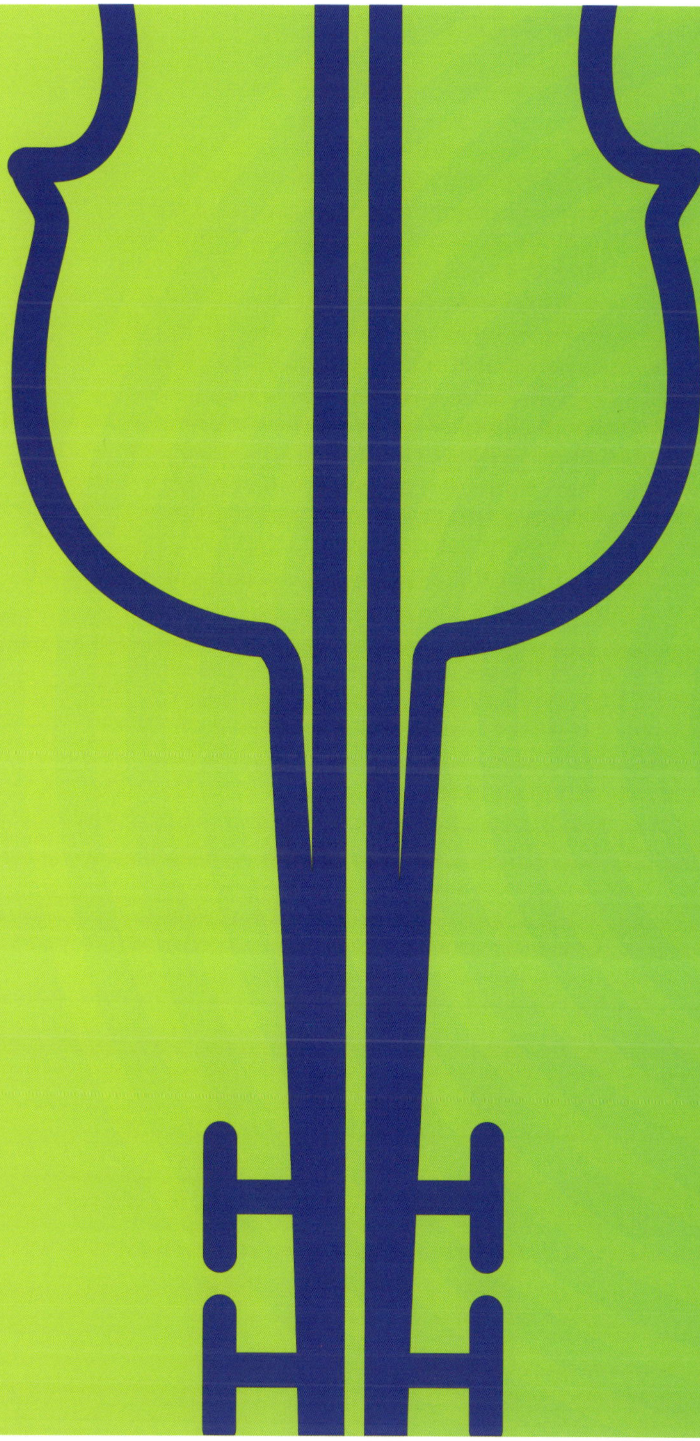

Scene 1: The Early Years

The story of the music and artists featured in Concerts from the Library of Congress is a rich and varied one, sometimes surprising and always compelling. In a sense, the identity of Concerts from the Library of Congress sprang fully formed from the minds of Elizabeth Sprague Coolidge and Carl Engel, chief of the Music Division. The first programs exhibited a core concept of what the concert series would embody: a cultural beacon that illuminates, Janus-like, the works of the past and the potential of the future. The early years of the concert series saw the establishment of standards and values befitting a world-class institution. Great musicians and scholars drew on the bedrock of the Library's collections to offer the public unprecedented free entrée to their worlds.

At the beginning of the concert series' history, the chief of the Music Division planned events in consultation with living donors: first Elizabeth Sprague Coolidge and later Gertrude Clarke Whittall. Over the years new programming formats and features were introduced to increase access to the Library's holdings and reach wider audiences. Eventually, the volume and complexity of event production necessitated a dedicated staff of specialists. However, many of the same considerations exist today as they did a century ago: artistic excellence, budget, content, variety, connections to the collections, and feasibility for the venue, to name a few.

A signature aspect of the Library's concert series is its persistent engagement with the Library's vast collections. In addition to music, books, correspondence, images, and other items, the Library also possesses an extraordinary collection of musical instruments. Whittall's gift of five priceless string instruments (given between 1935 and 1937) anchors the Library's instrument holdings, and the instruments have been a storied part of the Library's concert series since their arrival.

The visionary largesse of Coolidge and Whittall, combined with the Library's willingness to realize the

LIBRARY OF CONGRESS

FESTIVAL

OF

CHAMBER MUSIC

ELIZABETH SPRAGUE COOLIDGE FOUNDATION

PROGRAM

★ OCTOBER 28-29-30 ★ 1925 ★

WASHINGTON

Program cover for the inaugural Library of Congress Festival of Chamber Music held in the new hall October 28–30, 1925.

shared goal of a publicly accessible chamber music series, created a sustainable model of access and opportunity that persists today.

An Auspicious Beginning

At "8:45 o' clock" in the evening on October 28, 1925, Coolidge's dream of hearing music in a proper concert hall at the Library of Congress came to fruition in the Chamber Music Auditorium of the Library of Congress (its name officially changed to the "Coolidge Auditorium" in 1938, though its eventual title can be found in programs long before that year). Lynnwood Farnam was the first musician to perform in the new concert hall, offering a chorale prelude by J. S. Bach (1685–1750) on the organ ("To God on high all glory be," BWV 715). In a poetic gesture some twenty-eight years later, the memorial concert for Elizabeth Sprague Coolidge in 1953 concluded with organ music by Bach: the chorale prelude "Before your throne I now appear," BWV 668. If the Bach prelude at that first concert served as a nod to tradition, the Library's championing of new music was evident in the works that followed, newly composed for the occasion by Charles Martin Loeffler (1861–1931) and Frederick Stock (1872–1942).

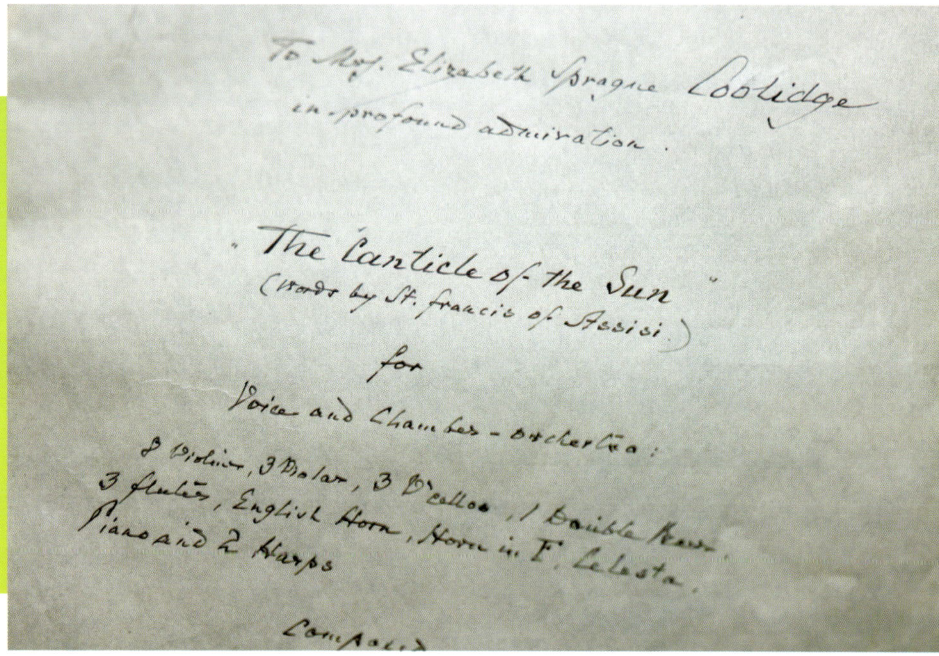

Top: Detail from opening page of Loeffler's work, here titled *Canticum fratris Solis* (Canticle to Brother Sun). This work and Frederick Stock's *Rhapsodic Fantasy* were composed especially for the Coolidge Auditorium's opening and were performed under the direction of Stock

Bottom: Detail from dedication page of Charles Martin Loeffler's *The Canticle of the Sun*, 1925..

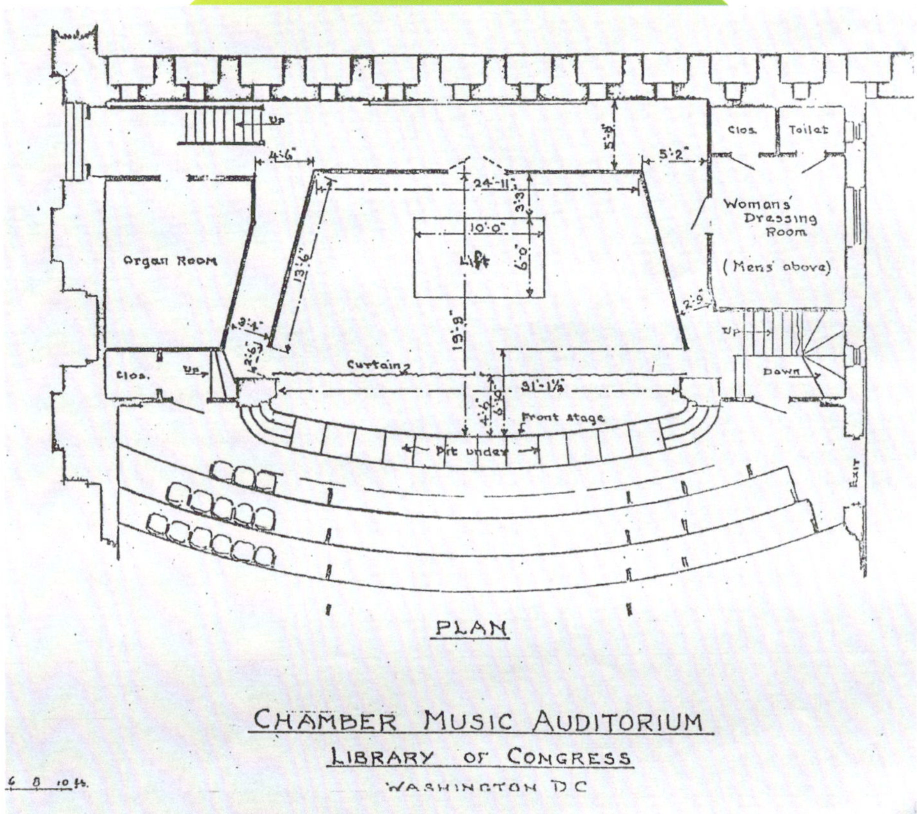

Early layout of the Coolidge Auditorium's stage and backstage areas, noting the organ room on stage right, undated. The E.M. Skinner organ's console could be shifted onstage for performance.

The constitutional framework of the series was further exhibited in the programming choices for the remaining concerts of the opening festival. The second concert was an all-Beethoven affair on the morning of the 29th, featuring the composer's op. 130 quartet played by the Festival Quartet of South Mountain, led by violinist William Kroll. In addition to string chamber music, the festival also featured other orchestral instruments: renowned flutist Georges Barrère joined Kroll and violinist Hugo Kortschak (in this instance on the viola) for a performance of Beethoven's Serenade, op. 25. Later that afternoon, the English Singers of London offered a selection of motets, madrigals, and folksongs (the latter arranged by Ralph Vaughan Williams), supplemented by English harpsichord music.

The inaugural chamber music festival closed on Elizabeth Sprague Coolidge's birthday, October 30, with a pair of concerts for strings, organ, and piano featuring the National String Quartet of Washington and the Chamber Music Society of San Francisco (filled with luminaries such as violinist Nathan Firestone and violinist/pianist/pedagogue Louis Persinger). The concerts again included modern works by composers Howard Hanson and Ildebrando Pizzetti alongside established classics. The festival ended with what must have been a revelatory experience for the audience: a performance of Franz Schubert's string quintet, D. 956, one of the great works of the string chamber music literature performed in a new American hall perfectly suited for such music. Thus concluded a chamber music festival that was packed to the trills with visionary artists and musical encounters of great cultural import.

Organic Offerings

While the Library eventually became known for its magnificent string and wind instrument collections, early visitors to a Coolidge Auditorium concert may have been struck by a grand instrument that is no longer there—a pipe organ. The organ played an essential role in early music performances, and in new music such as Paul Hindemith's *Kammermusik* no. 7. Major organists, including E. Power Biggs, were brought in for recitals and festivals, and for a time contributed greatly to the versatility of the space.

R. Nathaniel Dett, composer, pianist and educator, ca. 1910s. Dett was committed to exhibiting the versatility of African American musicians.

The 1925 E. M. Skinner organ was built for the auditorium and remained there until it was sold to Holy Trinity Catholic Church in Georgetown for $5,100 in July 1954. Despite its frequent appearance in the early decades of the concert series, Harold Spivacke (then chief of the Music Division) told Coolidge that the organ was seldom used and his efforts to arrange recitals were in vain. He called it "something of a white elephant." Some opinions held that the organ produced too much sound for the hall. It was determined that it should have a second life in another venue that could make better use of it. The "king of instruments" had gone from an integral to a vestigial organ.

Nathaniel Dett and the Hampton Institute Choir

African American performers made their first appearance at the Library during the second season, with the December 17, 1926, performance of the Hampton Institute Choir—an a cappella group of eighty singers that was among the largest choirs ever to assemble in the Coolidge Auditorium. The choir was under the direction of celebrated composer and pianist Dr. R. Nathaniel Dett (1882–1943).

The cultural significance of the event cannot be overstated; the federal workforce at the time was racially segregated and would remain so until a 1948 executive order from President Truman prohibited the practice. The concert was a great success, with Washington's *Evening Star* raving the next day about the quality of the performers and the audience's response to the concert: "This choir is made up of young people of high school and college age, and the clarity and sureness of their *a capella* [sic] work in even eight-part mixed chorus are things at which to marvel." The audience "...refused to go home at the end of the program until two encores had been given, and then went with reluctance." The *Washington Times-Herald* of December 19 extolled, "America is rich in a fundamental thing when such art can be produced by the youth among us. The visit of the Hampton Institute Choir writes a page of musical history of which we are justly proud."

The choir's program included primarily sacred music, including works by Dett himself, hymns, Christmas carols, and spirituals such as "Swing Low, Sweet Chariot" and "Deep River." The person behind their performance at the Library seems to have been Elizabeth Sprague Coolidge, who had visited the campus and met with Dett. In a letter to her on October 2, 1926, Dett noted that,

> *I am supposing that you would like a program similar to the one which we arranged for you when you were at Hampton. Possibly you will recall that we sang one or two compositions of mine at that time. Since then I have written a new anthem which we expect to include on our program in Washington; the anthem is based on a Negro theme and the object of this letter is to request that in consideration of the opportunity that you are making for us, that I be permitted to dedicate the work to you.*

Coolidge's response is unknown, and it is unclear if the new anthem was performed at the Library, but what is certain is that Dett's impact has been long lasting. His work at the Hampton Institute and beyond continues to inspire musicians around the world, who are indebted to the trailblazing artist. For instance, on April 13, 2007, the Library presented Canada's Nathaniel Dett Chorale, a living reminder of the music and values exhibited by its namesake.

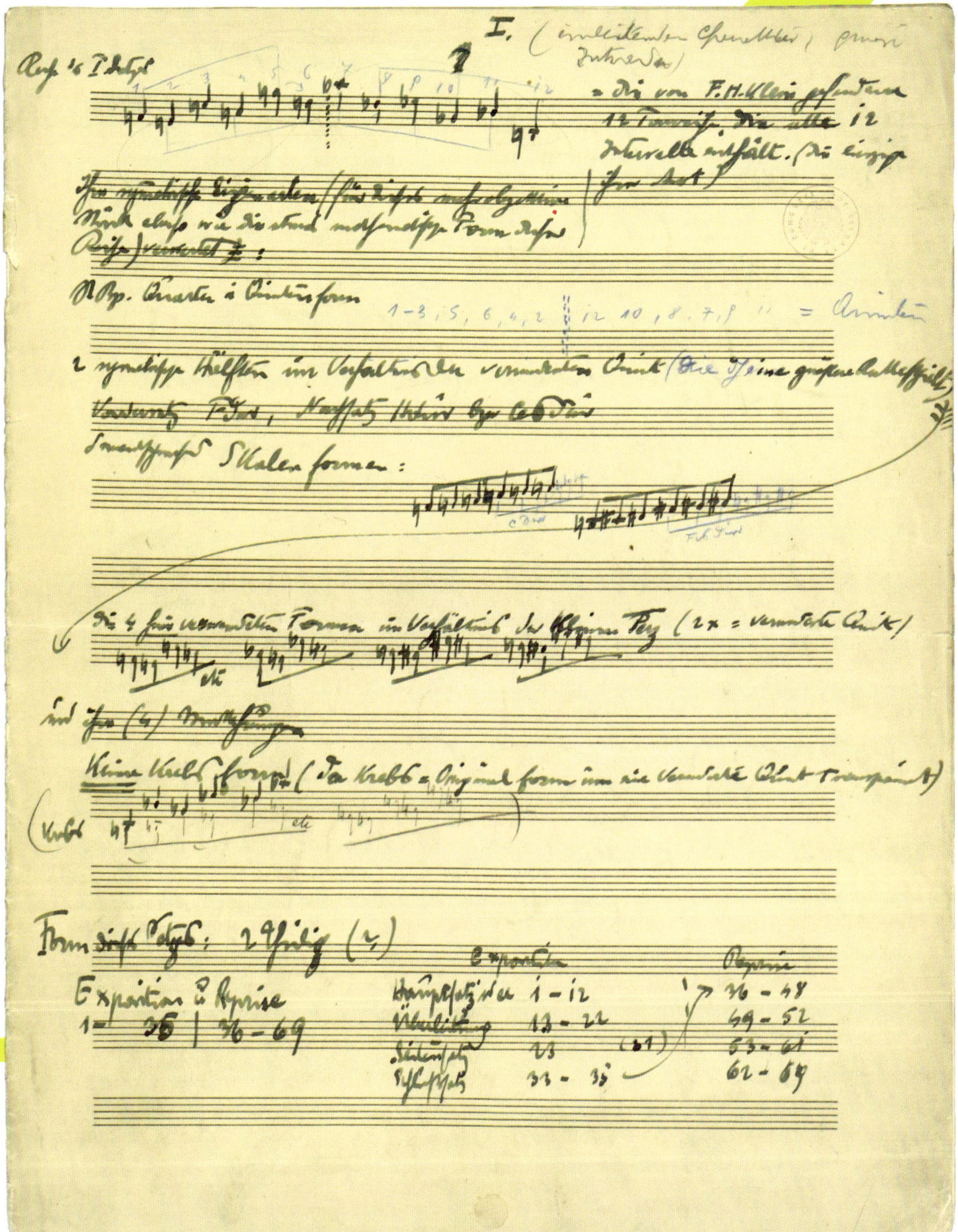

Alban Berg, holograph analysis of his *Lyric Suite*, page 1. Possibly prepared for Rudolf Kolisch, whose quartet premiered the work in 1927. An important resource for Berg studies, the Library also owns the holograph manuscripts of Berg's Violin Concerto and the opera *Wozzeck*.

Legends of the Hall

Even with the passage of time, the variety and quality of the concerts remained steady, punctuated by astounding clusters of activity realized within only a handful of days. The Coolidge Foundation sponsored one such festival April 7–9, 1935. It began with a program commemorating the 250th birthdays of J. S. Bach and George Frideric Handel, who shared the same birth year of 1685. Famed Irish American tenor John McCormack appeared alongside preeminent harpsichordist and musicologist Ralph Kirkpatrick with a chamber orchestra consisting of musicians from the Rochester Philharmonic, led by composer/conductor Howard Hanson.

In the late morning of April 8, 1935, the festival's second day, the Kolisch Quartet (known for their advocacy of modern music) performed three major works. They began with Beethoven's monumental op. 130 quartet, complete with the op. 133 *Grosse Fuge* finale. Next was Alban Berg's *Lyric Suite*; this performance took place just a few months before Berg's unexpected death due to complications from an insect sting at age 50. The concert closed with the premiere of Béla Bartók's String Quartet no. 5. An instant classic, this work had been commissioned by the Coolidge Foundation.

The Paris Instrumental Quintet (flute, harp, and string trio) gave another concert to close the packed day, playing recent works by Albert Roussell, Jean Cras, and Gian Francesco Malipiero. The Gordon String Quartet performed an all-American concert of music by Quincy Porter, Werner Janssen, and John Alden Carpenter (for whom a memorial concert would be held at the Library after his death in 1951). The final concert that evening was dedicated to the music of Igor Stravinsky (1882–1971) and included music (such as the string quartet *Concertino*) that would eventually be held in manuscript by the Library as part of its significant collection of the composer's works. Perhaps the most exciting element of the concert was the appearance of Stravinsky himself as one of the pianists.

Bloch to the Future: Composers at Play

In addition to Stravinsky, the Library's history is filled with other instances of major composers appearing onstage, as both instrumentalists and conductors. These artists have been drawn to the distinctive opportunity to perform outside of their primary focus areas in the inviting chamber music setting of the Coolidge Auditorium. On October 7, 1926, composer Ernest Bloch conducted pianist Arthur Loesser in a performance of the conductor's Concerto Grosso no. 1, among other pieces. Ottorino Respighi headlined a concert of his own music on February 21, 1927, in a performance that included his wife Elsa as the vocalist and the composer at the piano. Just a week later, the blind composer and multi-instrumentalist Edwin Grasse gave an organ recital. The eighth Festival of Chamber Music in 1937 included a concert on April 10 consisting entirely of music by Paul Hindemith, with the composer himself playing viola. Hindemith returned to the stage on the next day for a performance of his new viola concerto, *Der Schwanendreher*, under the direction of Mexican composer and conductor Carlos Chávez. In later years, composer-conductors continued to be featured in Library programming, including Charles Wuorinen in 2008, John Adams in 2013, and Oliver Knussen in 2014. These intimate interactions between creators and audiences have provided powerful experiences for Library patrons.

Ernest Bloch, at right, with Carl Engel, chief of the Music Division. Bloch, who conducted his own composition on the Library stage, was a favored composer of Elizabeth Sprague Coolidge. The Ernest Bloch collection at the Library of Congress started in 1925 with an initial tranche of materials placed on deposit.

Conductors on the Beat

Beyond composers, other major figures from the musical world have appeared on the Library's podium, attracted to the opportunity to perform in the Library's storied venue. Hans Kindler, cellist and founder of the National Symphony Orchestra, conducted the April 1928 performance that included the first version of Stravinsky's *Apollo* (called in that program "Apollo Musagetes"). Kindler appeared during that same festival as a cellist with flutist William Kincaid and composer/pianist Alfredo Casella. Conductor and pianist George Szell appeared with the celebrated Budapest Quartet and bassist Georges Moleux on May 16–17, 1946. Recordings of Szell's performance of Johannes Brahms and Franz Schubert quintets with the Budapest Quartet were released as part of Bridge Records' Great Performances from the Library of Congress series in 1996.

On October 9, 1929, renowned conductor Leopold Stokowski had his Library debut, conducting Hindemith's *Kammermusik* no. 7, op. 46, no. 2 with Lynnwood Farnam at the organ console. Stokowski later conducted the "Musicians from the Symphony of the Air" on November 17–18, 1960. The program included the string orchestra version of one of the Library's treasures: Arnold Schoenberg's *Verklärte Nacht* (1899). A recording of this event was issued in 1997 as part of the Bridge series.

Left: Conductor and cellist Hans Kindler with cello, between 1915 and 1920. Kindler appeared at the Library as cellist and conductor many times over the years. The Hans Kindler Foundation Trust Fund was formed in his honor in 1984 to support concerts that feature the cello.

Right: Caricature of Leopold Stokowski by Miguel Covarrubias, 1925. The Library has several of Stokowski's arrangements in manuscript, including the version of Modest Mussorgsky's *Night on Bald Mountain* used for Walt Disney Studio's *Fantasia* in 1940.

Entering the Strad-o-sphere

by Paul Allen Sommerfeld, Senior Music Reference Specialist

Gertrude Clarke Whittall, ca. 1950.

In the early years of the concert series, performances were occasionally funded by sources beyond Elizabeth Sprague Coolidge's foundation, including the Friends of Music (a community-based organization whose funds were later transferred into a Library trust fund), and the occasional one-off concert supported by an individual, such as Mary Louise Curtis Bok, founder of the Curtis Institute of Music. In the 1930s, the Coolidge fortune was not immune to the devastation of the Great Depression, leaving room for new endowments to buttress the Library's burgeoning series. A transformative new fund emerged in 1936, and the Gertrude Clarke Whittall Foundation quickly donned the mantle of a twin supportive pillar of the series, alongside the Coolidge Foundation.

Gertrude Clarke Whittall (1867–1965) inaugurated her extensive Library-focused philanthropic efforts when she gifted the Music Division four Stradivari instruments in 1935—two violins, one viola, and one violoncello—acquired largely through the efforts of violinist Louis Krasner (a third violin arrived in 1937). Antonio Stradivari (1644–1737) is perhaps the best known master Cremonese instrument maker. His stringed instruments are renowned for their craftsmanship and revered for their tone. At her express wish, the "Strads" were to be played because "in no other way could they be heard and kept alive." Whittall established her eponymous foundation in 1936 to ensure the instruments' ongoing care and to support concerts featuring them. She stipulated that the instruments not be removed from the Library except as necessary for maintenance. Whittall also gave the Library five bows, including three crafted by François Tourte (1737–1835), sometimes called the "Stradivari of the bow." Her gift to the American people followed in the footsteps of Coolidge's example, allowing all concertgoers the opportunity to hear these priceless instruments played by distinguished musicians.

The Whittall Foundation did not share the Coolidge Foundation's emphasis on commissioning and presenting new music; instead, the Whittall Foundation generally championed chamber works of the eighteenth, nineteenth, and early twentieth centuries. Whittall also supported augmenting the Library's radio broadcasts to maximize the foundation's concert audience. By the close of the series in 1937, CBS had received 1,031 letters from listeners in forty-six states and four Canadian provinces that substantiated "the complete dependence on radio of many music lovers for an opportunity to hear chamber music in any form."

In 1938, Whittall funded construction of the Whittall Pavilion to display the Strads. She continued to enlarge the foundation's endowment and, in 1941, established the Gertrude Clarke Whittall Foundation Collection of Autograph Musical Sources and Autograph Letters. The collection of Dr. Jerome Stonborough became the foundation's first addition, with manuscripts of Ludwig van Beethoven, Johannes Brahms, Wolfgang Amadeus Mozart, Franz Schubert, Clara Schumann, Richard Wagner, and Carl Maria von Weber. Subsequent significant additions included manuscripts, letters, and other ephemera of Joseph Haydn, Felix Mendelssohn, Niccolò Paganini, and Arnold Schoenberg.

Whittall's efforts blossomed into a unique fusion of artists, instruments, and holographs that encourage music performance combined with the study of primary sources. She stipulated, however, that these additional activities should remain secondary to the Strads' care and performance. Indeed, that focus laid the groundwork for expanding the Music Division's instrument collection, with the addition of rare violins, flutes, harpsichords, and more in the following decades. Moreover, Whittall's generosity did not end with the Music Division. In 1950 she created the Gertrude Clarke Whittall Poetry and Literature Fund to support the written and spoken word at the nation's Library.

On December 4, 1963, the commissioners of the District of Columbia honored Whittall with a citation for distinguished service to the American people. This recognition echoed her nascent hopes for the foundation. In a radio broadcast from December 18, 1937, Whittall had stated, "This collection of instruments ... belong to every one of you, for they are given to our government to hold and protect forever. ... They may be heard in concerts held in the Library, and through the medium of the radio, by an even larger audience. If the appreciation and enjoyment of music in America will be advanced thereby, the purpose of my gift will have been fulfilled." The seismic impact of Gertrude Clarke Whittall and her gift of five Stradivari instruments to the Library made it a major destination for connoisseurs of fine instruments.

Early configuration of the Whittall Pavilion, with Whittall's piano and glass Stradivari instrument case, ca. 1950s.

Another Instrumental Debut

Following closely on the heels of the arrival of Whittall's Stradivari quintet was the "Brookings" Amati violin. Made in 1654 by Nicolò Amati (1596–1684), the instrument was given to the Music Division in 1938 by Isabel Vallé Brookings, the widow of Robert Somers Brookings (founder of the Brookings Institution). The violin had been previously purchased by her husband in 1884 at the suggestion of Joseph Joachim, the renowned violinist and ardent friend of Johannes Brahms.

The Brookings Amati had its Library debut at a concert supported by the Nicholas Longworth Foundation on April 2, 1938. The mixed program was offered under the direction of none other than Nadia Boulanger, the esteemed pedagogue who helped train generations of composers from Igor Stravinsky and Elliott Carter to Aaron Copland, Philip Glass, and Quincy Jones. Her concert included works by composers as early as Claudio Monteverdi through living composers such as Theodore Chanler. A touching conclusion came in the form of the *Pie Jesu* by Boulanger's sister Lili, a talented composer who died young in 1918.

Beethoven at the Library

The Library swiftly established itself as a premiere American home for classical chamber music, buttressed by its growing arsenal of incredible string instruments. At the core of the repertoire was the music of Ludwig van Beethoven (1770–1827), whose string quartets have featured prominently throughout a century of programming. In 1927, the London String Quartet presented the Library's first cycle of all of Beethoven's string quartets. Later, such cycles would be heard nationwide, as in the 1935 CBS broadcast of the Pro Arte String Quartet of Brussels (during which audiences were asked to refrain from coughing). Other works have been frequently presented as well; celebrated interpretations from performers such as violinist Zino Francescatti and pianist/composer Robert Casadesus playing the violin sonatas to Hélène Grimaud performing the op. 109 piano sonata (held in manuscript at the Library) can be found throughout the series' history. At the Stradivari Bicentennial Festival in 1937, violinist Adolf Busch and pianist Rudolf Serkin performed a number of the Beethoven violin sonatas.

To celebrate the 250th anniversary of Beethoven's birth in 2020, the Library presented programs of various arrangements of his symphonies. Produced for a virtual audience during the COVID-19 pandemic, the project included one performance by the four-hand piano team ZOFO, which could be experienced via a special augmented reality app that allowed users to place themselves at different spots in the "virtual hall" relative to the performers. Christopher Taylor also performed three of Franz Liszt's transcriptions of the Beethoven symphonies for solo piano. Available to the public online in perpetuity, the (Re)Hearing Beethoven Festival came replete with a 172-page program book with new commentary and analyses of the works.

Detail of violin by Nicolò Amati, Cremona, 1654, known as the "Brookings." The instrument was originally purchased by Robert Somers Brookings at the suggestion of violinist Joseph Joachim.

This page: Solo violin part from the opening of the third movement of Johannes Brahms's Violin Concerto, op. 77. Copyist manuscript with holograph annotations by Brahms and Joseph Joachim, 1879. Joachim's annotations on the violin part provide insight into the two musicians' back-and-forth discussion, and one can see where Brahms chose to accept or forego the advice of his friend. The Library also has the holograph manuscript score of Brahms' Violin Concerto.

Opposite page: Ludwig van Beethoven, sketch from the final movement of String Quartet in C-sharp minor, op. 131 (1825–6). Holograph manuscript. This sketch bears the affirmation of its authenticity in a note by composer and pianist Ferdinand Hiller at the bottom of the page.

Example 3

Beethoven/Liszt, Symphony no. 1 in C major, op. 21, I: mm.79-82 with "ossia"

A savvy performer recognizes the inherent musical value of both the primary text and Liszt's alternatives, making the choice at times a difficult one. When the choice occurs in the exposition and is repeated, the option is there to provide the alternative reading during the second pass, and this is something that Taylor does in his performance; on the first pass he plays the main text, then plays the ossia on the second:

Example 4

Beethoven/Liszt, Symphony no. 1 in C major, op. 21, I: mm.69-71 with ossia

The *ossia* passage is "closer" in attack profile to the fast string tremolos, but both settings have their merits. In other areas Liszt reserves the use of a particular choice of figuration that might otherwise have seemed like a "go-to" option for special moments (such as the repeated eighth-note octaves of measures 250-252, in lieu of *tremolando* 16th notes in the strings). These decisions have a dramatic impact on the flow of the work as a piano piece. Occasionally these kinds of changes occur in the main text, yielding a "deviant" but effective variation on the original. Consider the change in the violins to the new rhythm in Liszt's setting:

142

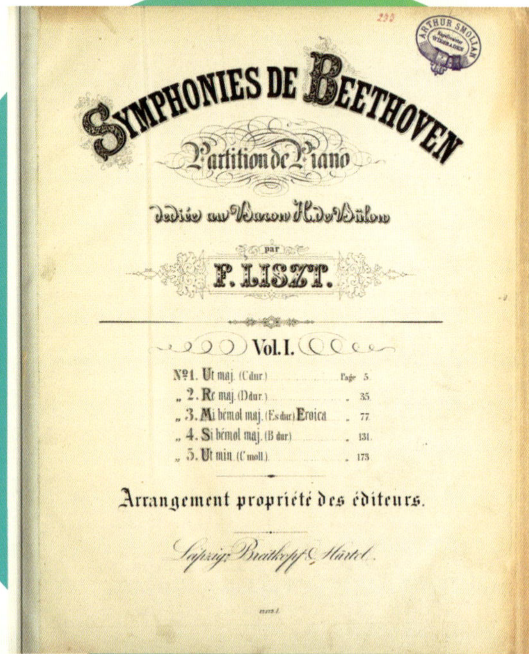
SYMPHONIES DE BEETHOVEN

Partition de Piano

dédiée au Baron H. de Bülow

par

F. LISZT.

Vol. I.

Nº1. Ut maj. (C dur)	Page	5.
„ 2. Ré maj. (D dur)		35
„ 3. Mi bémol maj. (Es dur) Eroica		77
„ 4. Si bémol maj. (B dur)		131
„ 5. Ut min (C moll)		173

Arrangement propriété des éditeurs.

Leipzig, Breitkopf & Härtel.

Above: Page from the Music Division's 2020 program book for the (Re)Hearing Beethoven Festival, with David Plylar's notes on Liszt's solo piano version of Beethoven's first symphony.

Right: Title page of first edition of Franz Liszt's transcriptions of Beethoven's symphonies for solo piano. Leipzig, Breitkopf und Härtel, 1865.

Commemorating the 13th Amendment

Late 1940 saw an extraordinary sequence of concerts organized in acknowledgment of the seventy-fifth anniversary of the passage of the Thirteenth Amendment to the US Constitution, which abolished slavery. A "Festival of Music," given under the auspices of the Whittall Foundation, focused on music both written by and performed by Black musicians.

The first concert on December 18, 1940, featured the singular soprano Dorothy Maynor, accompanied by Arpad Sandor in a program that included arias, Lieder, and mélodies from Handel to Charpentier. After the intermission, Maynor performed R. Nathaniel Dett's

"My Day," two songs by British composer Samuel Coleridge-Taylor, and a selection of Negro spirituals arranged by William Lawrence, Roland Hayes, and Dett, with whom Maynor had studied at the Hampton Institute.

The second concert of the festival was the Stradivari Memorial concert, an annual performance offered on the anniversary of Stradivari's death that employs the Library's magnificent string instruments. It featured Black European composers on the first half: two early quartets by the French composer Joseph Bologne, Chevalier de Saint-Georges, and the masterful clarinet quintet of Coleridge-Taylor. The Budapest String Quartet was joined by clarinetist Gustave Langenus for the quintet and paired the music with Antonín Dvořák's "American" quartet (op. 96).

A striking collection of commentators joined guitarist Joshua White and the Golden Gate Quartet in a sequence of lectures and performances of "Negro Folk Song." Alain Locke, a key figure of the Harlem Renaissance, spoke during the segment on spirituals. Poet and folklorist Sterling Brown (who would later be named poet laureate of his hometown of Washington, DC) led the section on blues and ballads. The final segment involved the Library's own Alan Lomax, who had famously interviewed Jelly Roll Morton on the Coolidge stage in 1938, in an exploration of reels and work songs. This kind of contextual programming remains a feature of many of the Library's concerts.

The final program of the series highlighted tenor Roland Hayes in a recital that paired Monteverdi with J. S. Bach and Robert Schumann's *Dichterliebe* alongside "African and Afro-American Songs and Folk Songs." Supported by pianist Reginald Boardman, Hayes closed the festival as one of the great ambassadors for universality in music, a particularly poignant stance in a still-segregated society.

From left: Dorothy Maynor, soprano, 1941. Maynor later performed at two presidential inaugurations (Truman, 1949, and Eisenhower, 1953), becoming the first African American singer to do so, and she founded the Harlem School of the Arts in 1964. Her breakout performances at the Berkshire Festival and with the Boston Symphony Orchestra in 1939 and 1940 were developed with the help of Serge Koussevitzky. • Samuel Coleridge-Taylor, composer, 1905. The Library holds several manuscripts of his compositions, including the *Ballade* in D minor, op. 4, for violin and orchestra (1895). • CD cover for *Freedom: The Golden Gate Quartet with Josh White*, part of the Great Performances from the Library of Congress series released in 2002 on Bridge Records. The disc includes the 1940 commentary from Sterling Brown, Alain Locke, and Alan Lomax. Dorothy Maynor's performance at the Library that year was also released by Bridge in 2002. • Roland Hayes, tenor and composer, January 29, 1954.

Scene 2: Residencies and Renown

The dark days before and during World War II drove many in the arts to seek sanctuary in the United States. Despite air raid instructions in the printed concert programs, Library audiences were thankfully free of the direct dangers engulfing the world. Some artists found musical opportunities at the Library of Congress, and pathways to stability crystallized as the implementation of residencies and additional major endowments gave an aura of permanence to the series. With Europe often not a viable option for performance opportunities during the war, the Library became venerated as a bastion of tradition and innovation for composers and performers.

During the war and in the early postwar period, Concerts from the Library of Congress settled into a variant of what evolutionary theorist Stephen Jay Gould might have described as "punctuated equilibrium," as the series exhibited dependably high-quality programming with flashes of brilliance taking it to new heights. The gravitational pull of the successful series continued to

Opposite page: A wrought iron gate featuring the shapes of violins leads from the Whittall Pavilion to the northwest courtyard of the Jefferson Building, January 2025. The cases housing some of the Library's Stradivari, Guarneri, and Amati instruments can be seen in the background. The Library's concerts serve as a gateway between the collections and the public.

Below: Detail from a 1942 Budapest String Quartet program with instructions in case the audience hears an air raid siren.

If an air raid alert is sounded during a concert, persons in the Coolidge Auditorium and the Whittall Pavilion will go to Shelter Area No. 4. This is reached by turning left on leaving the lobby of the Coolidge Auditorium or the ante-room of the Whittall Pavilion and descending the center stairways in the front of the building to the cellar. Then follow the signs pointing to Shelter Area No. 4. All lights will be extinguished temporarily five minutes after the air raid horns have sounded.

engage more donors, instruments, and artists excited to perform in the renowned space.

In addition to classical chamber music, other genres, such as newly composed concert music and jazz, also connected audiences with the Library's holdings. Major figures, such as Serge Koussevitzky, partnered with the Library to further enrich its status as a cultural force in the world. Whether historic or modern, the Library's acquisitions helped to sculpt the programming, and the dedication of its leadership, staff, and resident ensembles underpinned the concert series' legacy of excellence.

A Hungarian Rhapsody

Joseph Szigeti (1892–1973), one of the great violinists of the twentieth century, performed Beethoven's famously challenging "Kreutzer" sonata with Alfred Cortot at the Founder's Day concert on October 30, 1926—the first so called in honor of Elizabeth Sprague Coolidge's birthday. But it was Szigeti's appearance with his Hungarian compatriot Béla Bartók at the piano in April 1940 that became the stuff of legend. The program opened with the "Kreutzer" sonata, followed by the Debussy violin sonata and Bartók's Rhapsody no. 1, closing after the break with Bartók's second violin sonata. The recital by Bartók and Szigeti was a long time in the making; the publicly anti-fascist Bartók sought to leave Europe in the volatile political landscape of 1939, and his correspondence with Music Division Chief Harold Spivacke reveals that he was worried about his family and his country. He wrote,

> *I wonder if you know our situation here? We see that small countries are invaded from one day to another quite unexpectedly by the most terrible armies and subjected to tortures of every kind. As for my own country, now, instead of one dangerous neighbor, we have got two of them; nobody knows what will happen the next day. It may happen, if I leave my country for America, that I can't return, can't even have news from my family.*

Correspondence with Spivacke covers details of the program coming together and the logistics of booking Bartók's passage to the United States. Ultimately Bartók was not only able to perform at the Library, but was able to immigrate to the United States later that year; he lived in the United States for the remainder of his life.

Bela Bartok, 1922.

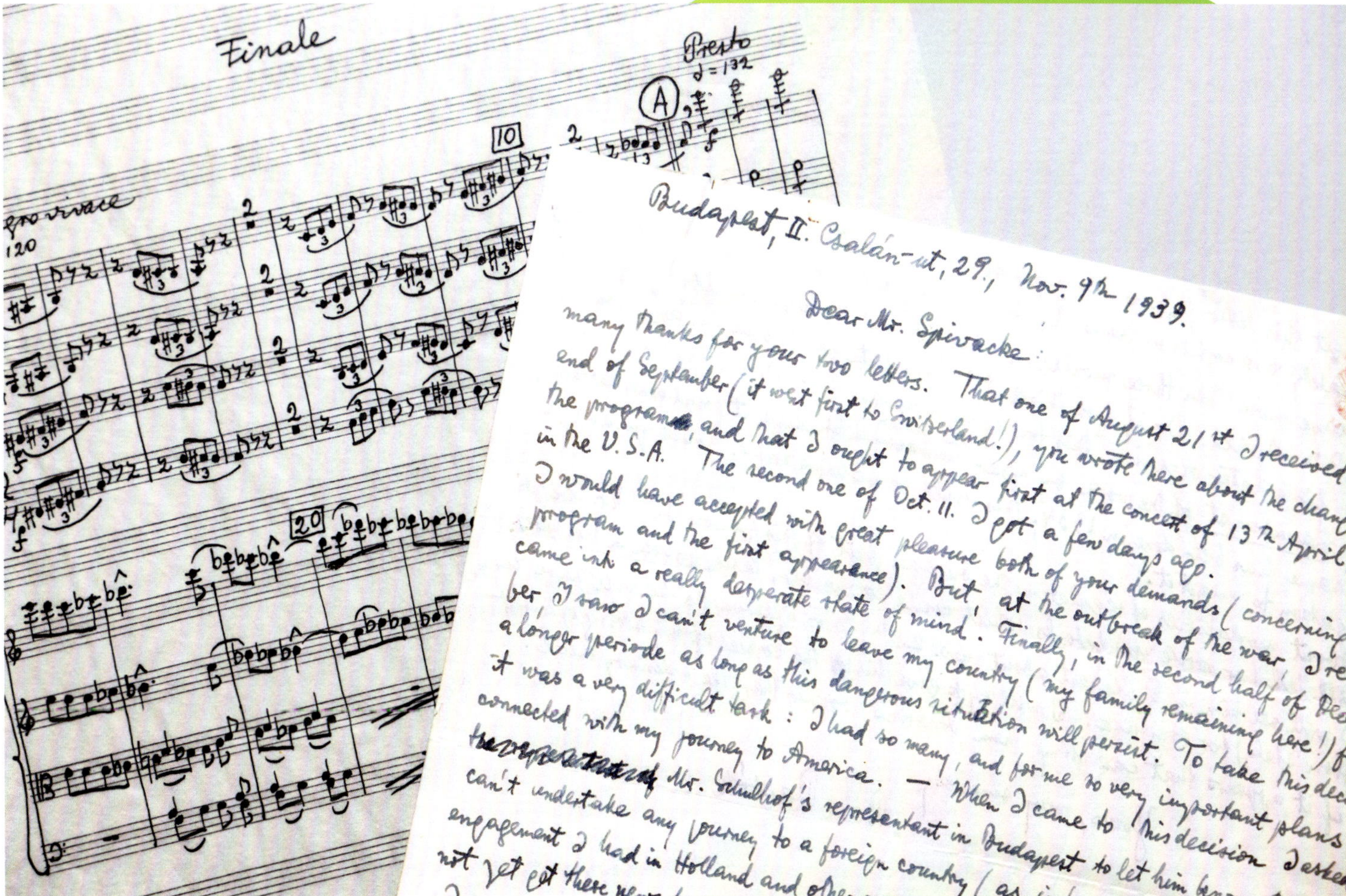

Szigeti continued to advocate for his friend after their landmark performance at the Library, lauding Koussevitzky for commissioning Bartók's *Concerto for Orchestra* (held in manuscript at the Library) and encouraging the influential conductor to perform more of his music, as Bartók suffered from poor health at the end of his life. Szigeti wrote in part that "If you should decide to give his 'Music for Strings[, Percussion] and Celesta' the performance that only you and your orchestra can give of such an exquisite tonal texture, that would be not only a great artistic deed but also an act of healing!"

Page one of a holograph letter from Béla Bartók to Harold Spivacke, November 9, 1939, atop the opening page of the Finale from the holograph manuscript of Bartók's fifth string quartet. Personal correspondence is often displayed at related performances, offering a glimpse of the "human" side of revered figures like Bartók.

Artist Residencies

Anne E. McLean, Senior Producer for Concerts and Special Projects

For a significant portion of its history, Concerts from the Library of Congress featured multiple yearly appearances of select artists in residence. Funded by various sources, the residencies were initially inspired by the desire to allow ensembles to master the Library's Stradivari instruments. Residencies offer artists and ensembles a formal artistic collaborator relationship with the concert series, with recurring appearances and a curatorial role in developing programs.

The Library's influential artist residencies greatly amplified its reputation in the cultural realm, nationally and internationally. Among the legendary artists that have appeared in the Coolidge Auditorium, four have served as long-term artists-in-residence, including the Budapest and Juilliard String Quartets, the Beaux Arts Trio, and artists appearing in the Summer Chamber Festivals that blossomed in the 1980s.

Left: Budapest String Quartet in performance at the Library, 1938. The Library's first resident ensemble, the Budapest Quartet developed a consistent soundworld using the Stradivari instruments.

Opposite page: Then a US representative, John F. Kennedy wrote to Music Division Chief Harold Spivacke, requesting tickets to the Budapest String Quartet concert on March 21, 1952.

JOHN F. KENNEDY
11TH DIST., MASSACHUSETTS

COMMITTEES:
EDUCATION AND LABOR
DISTRICT OF COLUMBIA

Congress of the United States
House of Representatives
Washington, D. C.

March 14, 1952

Mr. Harry Spivacke, Chief
Music Division
The Library of Congress
Washington 25, D. C.

Dear Mr. Spivacke:

I wonder if it would be possible to include my name on the list of those to whom announcements are sent, regarding the various concerts which are presented at the Library of Congress.

Specifically, I am most anxious to secure two tickets to the concert being given by the Budapest String Quartet on Friday, March 21st, in the Coolidge Auditorium of the Library, and shall be most grateful to you for any consideration you may be able to give my request.

Thanking you in advance for your kindness, and with best wishes, I am,

Sincerely yours,

John Kennedy

make cards
send for 3/27

3/22

"Well, we felt, all four of us, specially honored—my God!—to be at the Library of Congress, that was really like you were becoming the Prime Ministers, you know, or... in the cabinet...and also to have five incredible instruments...we were very proud to play them. It was really very special."

–Budapest String Quartet violinist Alexander Schneider

In 1938 the Budapest Quartet played the Library's Stradivari instruments for the first time; two years later, remaining in America during World War II, the musicians accepted a residency under the auspices of the Whittall Foundation. The Budapest residency would last twenty-two years, become a model for other major concert presenters, and take the Library's concert series to vast radio audiences nationwide. "As a teenager in Portland [Oregon], I used to listen to those wonderful broadcasts of chamber music from the Library of Congress, to think and dream...that would be the life for me," said violinist Robert Mann, founder of the Juilliard String Quartet (JSQ). His dream would become part of the Library's history, as the quartet—"America's quartet," according to critic Mark Swed—began a new residency in the fall of 1962. Already a favorite with Library audiences from appearances as early as 1948, the Juilliard Quartet would now be the home team, playing the Library's Strads in more than 560 concerts over a four-decade tenure.

The Juilliard's tremendous energy, their bold, exciting performances, and their passionate engagement with new music galvanized audiences. They championed a long list of important American composers including Aaron Copland, Samuel Barber, Henry Cowell, Elliott Carter—who received two Library of Congress commissions, including his Quintet for piano and string quartet—Ruth Crawford Seeger, Milton Babbitt, and a host of others. As with the Budapest, JSQ featured an all-star lineup of guest artists, including figures such as Jorge Bolet, Leonard Bernstein, Walter Trampler, and Claudio Arrau.

In 1982, the newly established William and Adeline Croft Fund placed the Library in the enviable position of hosting residencies for two of the world's most sought-after ensembles. Like the JSQ, the Beaux Arts Trio had drawn an ardent Library fanbase since its Coolidge Auditorium debut in 1958. Throughout its existence the trio was anchored by the extraordinary pianist Menahem Pressler, who also performed at the Library over the decades as a soloist. Pressler partnered as well with the cellist János Starker and as a guest artist with good friends in the Juilliard, Emerson, and other quartets. The Coolidge, Whittall, and McKim funds later supported concerts by the trio after its formal residency ended in 2003, making possible a fifty-year history at the Library that would conclude with the Beaux Arts Trio's farewell season in 2008.

Miles Hoffman—violist, author, and radio commentator—founded the fourth residency for the concert series in 1982. The popular Summer Chamber Festival was anchored by a group of musicians (later known as the American Chamber Players) that continued for the better part of a decade. As artistic director, Hoffman's humor, charm, and enthusiastic exploration of the Library's music collections enlivened a flourishing multievent festival featuring talented young performers. Memorable moments included a two-piano performance of Igor Stravinsky's *Le Sacre du printemps* (June 19, 1984, performed by Barbara Weintraub and Hugh Wolff) and an excellent thirteen-person conductor-less performance of the suite from Aaron Copland's *Appalachian Spring* (June 27, 1989). Festival concerts were broadcast in a standalone Library of Congress radio series, and a number of performances were captured and released in critically acclaimed recordings.

The residencies eventually ended to make space for a broader variety of performances, but the notion of mini-residencies remains an attractive way to present more repertoire economically. In these cases, musical groups typically stay a few days to offer a sampling of works. Early examples are the appearances by the Roth String Quartet in February 1934 that included works by a range of composers from Walter Piston to Roy Harris, all paired with pieces by Mozart. The same principle would be echoed frequently over the years by quartets ranging from the Coolidge Quartet to the Flux Quartet. Engagements of this type allow for concentrated bursts of repertoire, and in the cases where musicians are using the Library's Stradivari instruments, it allows more time for the artists to adapt to the instruments' idiosyncrasies.

Sometimes outside curation would come into play, with special short-term residencies designed in part by figures such as John Adams, Rosanne Cash, Oliver Knussen, and Maria Schneider. Schneider's Library commission *Data Lords* (2016), that was premiered as part of her mini-residency, would eventually be a part of her Grammy-winning album of the same name (her work was also a finalist for the 2021 Pulitzer Prize).

Top: Juilliard String Quartet, performing on the Coolidge stage in 1962. The Juilliard String Quartet regularly advocated for living composers in their programming, bringing audiences in regular contact with contemporary music alongside more traditional fare. Like the Budapest String Quartet, the Juilliard players were avid baseball fans who often dashed offstage between pieces to check out incoming updates on World Series scores.

Middle: The Beaux Arts Trio performs at the Tanglewood Music Festival, Lenox, Massachusetts, July 10, 1986.

Bottom: Rosanne Cash performing in the Coolidge Auditorium as part of her residency, which included multiple events curated by the artist, December 5, 2013.

Early Music at the Library

Classical and Romantic-era chamber music have always featured prominently in the Library's concert programming, but since its inception the series has also been a haven for music from the Baroque era and before, and major figures in the field quickly found their way to the Coolidge stage. For Founder's Day in 1927, the preeminent harpsichord virtuosa Wanda Landowska performed Mozart's A-major sonata (K. 331) at the piano. The remainder of the program included works such as Bach's "Italian Concerto," BWV 971, and a Domenico Scarlatti sonata at the harpsichord.

Beyond foundational titans such as Landowska and Ralph Kirkpatrick, the Library has presented many specialists in early keyboard music. Modern masters including Christophe Rousset (sometimes with Les Talens Lyriques) and Kristian Bezuidenhout have appeared in numerous guises. The work of multi-instrumentalist keyboard artists such as Bezuidenhout and Benjamin Alard—an artist who has recorded all of Bach's keyboard music on harpsichord, clavichord, and organ, and who gave two recitals on clavichord and harpsichord at the Library in December 2022—is given an inherent boost by the auditorium's ability to propagate the sound of low-volume instruments throughout the space.

Left: Wanda Landowska, harpsichordist, ca. 1920–25. In 2004, two of Landowska's weighty Pleyel harpsichords came to the Library, as well as the Wanda Landowska/Restout Memorial Fund.

Right: Detail of one of Wanda Landowska's Pleyel harpsichords held at the Library of Congress. The idiosyncratic instruments have been played by artists including Skip Sempe, Mitzi Meyerson, and Mahan Esfahani.

Larger Baroque ensembles also feature in the Library's concerts. Sometimes the programming is historically mirrored: over the course of two concerts in April 1939, Feri Roth led the National Symphony Orchestra and harpsichordist Alice Ehlers in a performance of all six *Brandenburg Concertos* of Bach—a feat that would be matched in a single concert by the Freiburg Baroque Orchestra in 2014.

Jordi Savall and others have appeared multiple times with exploratory ensembles, aimed at broadening the canon of early music to be more inclusive of various cultures. They are part of a long Library tradition of support for early music that has featured influential artists, including Noah Greenberg and his group New York Pro Musica, ensembles with countertenor Alfred Deller, and Pro Musica Antiqua of Brussels with Safford Cape. Many of these groups were led by significant harpsichordists such as Gustav Leonhardt and later Masaaki Suzuki, whose distinguished ensemble Bach Collegium Japan performed multiple times on the series. Vocal ensembles have also provided audiences with access to pre-Baroque music, with groups such as Stile Antico, the Tallis Scholars, and Ars Nova Copenhagen performing unaccompanied gems from the repertoire. With respect to the use of authentic instruments and tunings, the Library is catholic in its presentation of early music styles and instruments, opting to present a variety of perspectives.

Serge Koussevitzky Partners with the Library

by Kate Rivers, Senior Music Specialist, Music Division

One of the figures who looms large in the history of performances and commissions at the Library of Congress is conductor and patron of music Serge Koussevitzky (1874–1951). His legacy was preserved at the Library starting in 1949, but his relationship with the institution and its advocates began much earlier. When Koussevitzky arrived in the United States by way of Paris in 1924 to assume the role of conductor and music director of the Boston Symphony Orchestra (BSO), he was already a star, known throughout Europe and Russia as a virtuoso performer on the double bass and an electrifying conductor on the podium, as well as a fierce champion of contemporary composers and new music. Thanks to family wealth inherited by his wife Natalie, Koussevitzky's personal philanthropy as a publisher and commissioner of new works had already shaped the modern musical landscape with his support of composers such as Sergei Rachmaninoff, Alexander Scriabin, and Igor Stravinsky.

Following Koussevitzky's appointment to the BSO, regular orchestra concerts in the nation's capital soon acquainted him with the Library of Congress, where he developed a cordial relationship with Music Division staff. In a breathless 1927 telegram, Music Division Chief Carl Engel urged Koussevitzky to "take lunch" with him at the Library right away, as he was "anxious" for him to see a newly acquired Robert Schumann manuscript. As early as 1930, Engel reminded Koussevitzky that he had "promised...one of [his] autograph manuscripts for [the Library's] notable collection," indicating that acquiring Koussevitzky's important archive was already on the minds of Music Division personnel.

Koussevitzky conducted players from the BSO in a 1933 Coolidge Foundation Festival of Chamber Music program, demonstrating his support for the Library's famous patron as well as his embrace of American composers by programming the young Aaron Copland's *Music for the Theatre*. It was perhaps his and his wife Natalie's evolving friendship with Coolidge herself that cemented Koussevitzky's

| Serge Koussevitzky, conductor, ca. 1930s.

Left: Initialed pre-publication draft of *Koan* from 2023 by Hilda Paredes. Commissioned by the Koussevitsky Foundation, *Koan* was performed at the Library by the Takt Trio on May 17, 2024, along with a new Verna and Irving Fine Endowment commission by Marcos Balter (*Atlas*, 2024).

Opposite page: Holograph title page and excerpt with housing of Olivier Messiaen's *Turangalîla-Symphonie* (1948). In addition to chamber works suitable for the Coolidge Auditorium, the Koussevitzky Foundation has commissioned large-scale works such as *Turangalîla* and Benjamin Britten's opera *Peter Grimes* (1945).

connection to the Library, as her arts patronage and philanthropic endeavors complemented his own practices. Over numerous meals and at concerts in Washington, Boston, and in the Berkshire mountains where the Tanglewood Music Center would blossom, the bond between the Koussevitzkys and Coolidge grew especially strong.

Koussevitzky formalized his commissioning activities through his foundation in 1942, with each new work bearing a dedication to his late wife Natalie. As the number of important manuscripts in his possession continued to grow, Koussevitzky wrote to Music Division Chief Harold Spivacke in 1948, "the question of a permanent home for the manuscripts...is of much concern to me." With Spivacke's steady guidance, a repository for Koussevitzky's valuable collection—as well as an institutional framework for carrying on his critical work supporting composers—took shape. The Serge Koussevitzky Music Foundation in the Library of Congress was established in 1949, inaugurated at a festive luncheon hosted by Library benefactor Gertrude Clarke Whittall. Koussevitzky wrote that "the establishment of the new Foundation gives me great satisfaction and a feeling of confidence that the work in which I have had so great an interest will be effectively continued." A substantial portion of the Library's commissions have been administered through the Koussevitzky Foundation, which proudly carries on the vision of its legendary namesake.

The Providential Pairing of Whittall and Schoenberg

In addition to commissioning, the Library acquires significant primary sources through copyright deposits, the acumen of acquisitions experts, and the generosity of donors. An especially good example of this latter path is the case of Arnold Schoenberg (1874–1951) and Gertrude Clarke Whittall.

Although "new music" was largely the domain of Coolidge, Whittall's funding was nevertheless pivotal in preserving aspects of music history for the Library and the world at large. The Library's interactions

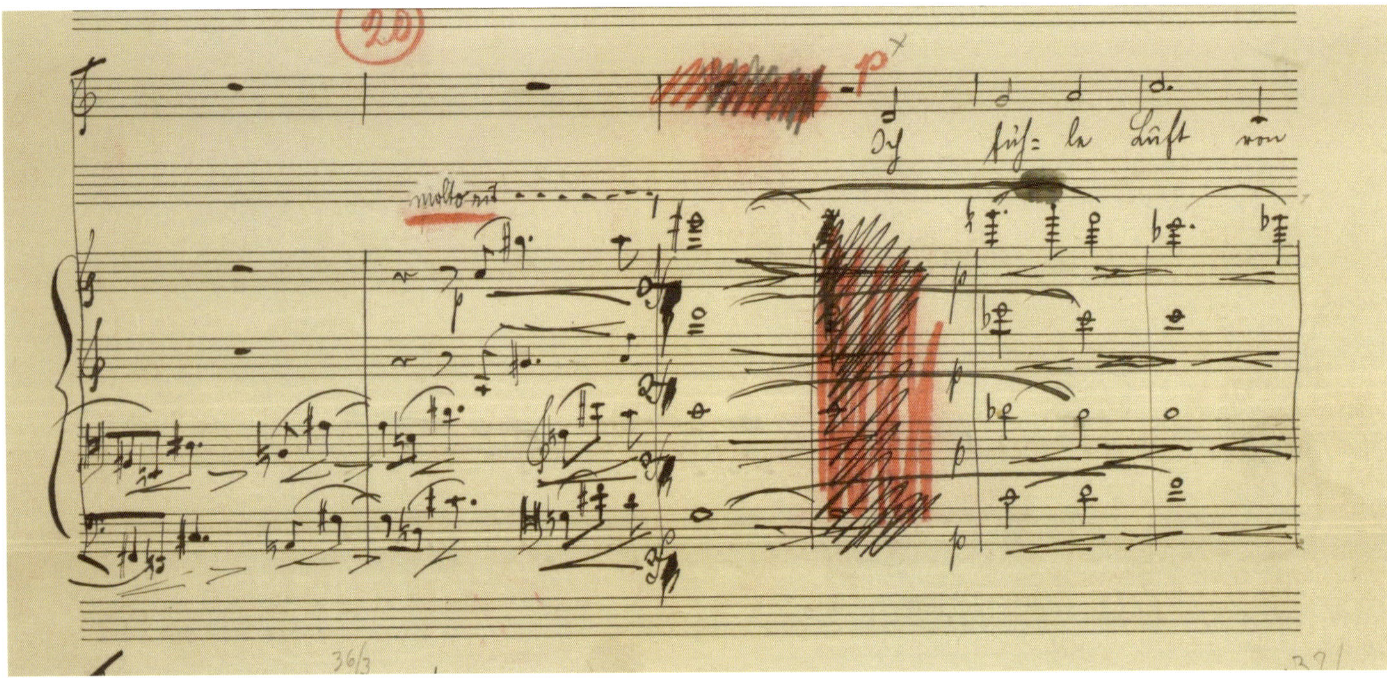

Top: Detail from the magical closing bars of Arnold Schoenberg's *Verklärte Nacht*, holograph manuscript. **Bottom:** Arnold Schoenberg, String Quartet no. 2, op. 10, fourth movement ("Entrückung," Stefan George), p. 34, detail, at the famous first entrance of the voice in the final movement. This piece moved away from the familiar world of traditional tonal harmony, and Schoenberg's setting of lines such as "Ich fühle Luft von anderem Planeten" (I feel air from other planets) gave a poetic impetus to the bold new paths that Schoenberg would traverse in the coming years.

with composer Arnold Schoenberg in 1950 offer an example of a time when the strands of patronage, performance, and preservation came together to everyone's advantage. Schoenberg had long been a friend of the Library and was the recipient of three commissions: the Elizabeth Sprague Coolidge Foundation commissioned his third and fourth string quartets in 1927 and 1936, and the Koussevitzky Music Foundation commissioned *A Survivor from Warsaw* in 1947.

At the end of Schoenberg's life, amid financial pressures and the desire to preserve his legacy after the cultural and literal devastation of the Second World War, he sold three of his most iconic compositions to the Library via the Whittall Foundation. The holograph manuscript of *Verklärte Nacht* ("Transfigured Night") from 1899 was the earliest work in the batch. This string sextet, written in response to Richard Dehmel's poetry, is perhaps his most performed work and shows Schoenberg at the height of his powers in the realm of chromatic harmony.

Also included in the purchase was the second string quartet, which Schoenberg composed in 1907–8. The second quartet stands out for many reasons, including Schoenberg's inclusion of a voice to sing the poetry of Stefan George in two of the movements, "Litanei" and "Entrückung." In addition to the holograph manuscript, Schoenberg included one of the first printed editions of the quartet, initially published in a small quantity at his expense, with the following inscription:

> *To Mrs. Gertrude Clarke Whittall, whose generosity made it possible to place the three manuscripts of mine:* Verklärte Nacht, Zweites Streichquartett *[second string quartet] and* Pierrot lunaire *in such an honorable manner and who through her donation procured me this highly dignified reimbursement.*
>
> *In thankfulness, Arnold Schoenberg, September 27, 1950*

No less important was the third holograph score in the purchase: the epochal *Pierrot lunaire* from 1912, a setting of twenty-one poems Schoenberg selected from a set of fifty by Albert Giraud in the tradition of the Italian *commedia dell'arte*. This melodrama for voice and ensemble served as a calling card for post-Romantic expressionism. Its influence on other composers has been immeasurable.

Thanks to the generosity of forward-looking patrons like Whittall, these works and others that have come to the Library of Congress can now be performed here in the presence of their holograph manuscripts, perhaps contextualized by new notes, editions, or analyses that have emerged from the public's access to these foundational documents. Schoenberg's music continues to captivate on the Coolidge stage. Soprano Tony Arnold and the Orion String Quartet performed the second quartet on April 8, 2017, and on March 15, 2019, mezzo-soprano Rachel Calloway and Ensemble Signal performed *Pierrot lunaire* with Brad Lubman conducting. In a two-concert festival in October 2024, for the 150th anniversary of Schoenberg's birth, Quatuor Diotima performed Schoenberg's complete string quartets, with the exception of the second—all of which are held in manuscript at the Library. On December 6, 2024, the Experiential Orchestra performed *Verklärte Nacht* on the Coolidge Auditorium stage in its string orchestra version with an additional new text by Ling Ling Huang.

Ancient Voices and Modern Music

A signature moment for new music took place on the afternoon of Halloween in 1970. It was the central day of the Fourteenth Festival of Chamber Music supported by the Elizabeth Sprague Coolidge Foundation—a series of forward-looking concerts that included many kinds of newly composed music with electronics, such as a work for "tape alone" (Charles Dodge's computer-synthesized *Changes*); a work for soprano, violin, and four-track tape (Mel Powell's *Cantilena*); and an early appearance of the Moog synthesizer (in John Eaton's *Mass*). The festival also included a survey of acoustic works by various composers, including Luigi Dallapiccola and Milton Babbitt. Almost as a kind of playful bait, the music of Beethoven was sprinkled throughout, with excerpts

Above: Jay Williams with a Moog synthesizer in the Coolidge Auditorium as part of the 14th Festival of Chamber Music in October, 1970.

Right: Signed program from the Fourteenth Festival of Chamber Music, October 30–November 1, 1970. Artists have signed copies of most programs presented at the Library since the concert series' early days.

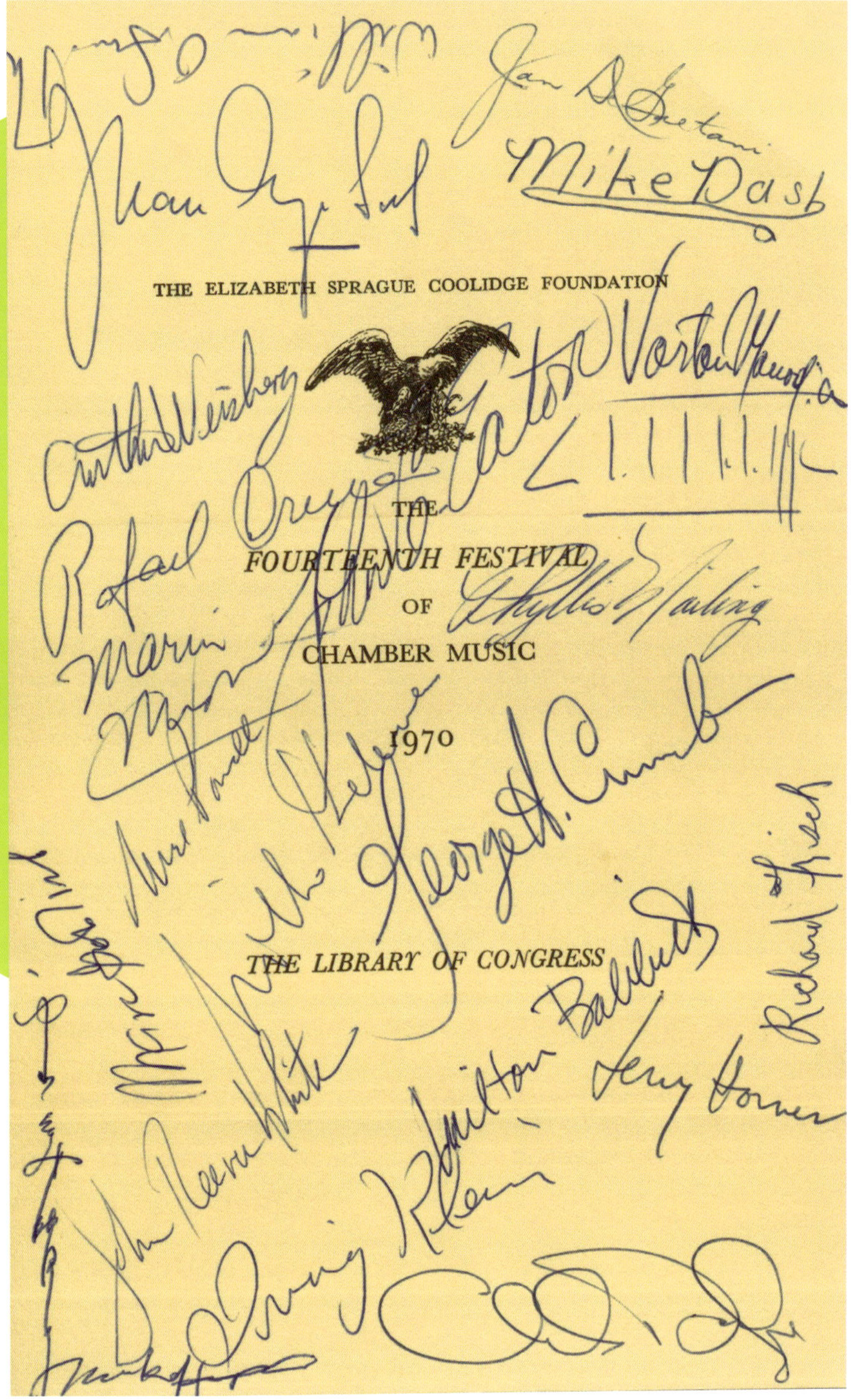

THE ELIZABETH SPRAGUE COOLIDGE FOUNDATION

THE

FOURTEENTH FESTIVAL

OF

CHAMBER MUSIC

1970

THE LIBRARY OF CONGRESS

from *The Creatures of Prometheus* to the wind octet (op. 103) making an appearance, and violinist Nathan Milstein performing three of the violin sonatas.

Couched in the program on that Saturday afternoon was the world premiere of George Crumb's *Ancient Voices of Children*, featuring the brilliant soprano Jan DeGaetani and the boy soprano Michael Dash. The Nonesuch recording of the work the following year received three Grammy nominations. Commissioned by the Elizabeth Sprague Coolidge Foundation, *Ancient Voices of Children* brought the musical world of Crumb to a broader audience, showcasing his unique voice and intense readings of Federico García Lorca's poetry. It was not the first or last commission Crumb would receive from the Library (*Madrigals, Books I and II* was a Koussevitzky commission from 1964, and *Kronos–Kryptos* was co-commissioned by the Verna and Irving Fine Endowment in 2019). In the final years of his life, Crumb—who died in 2022—donated his papers to the Library, where researchers

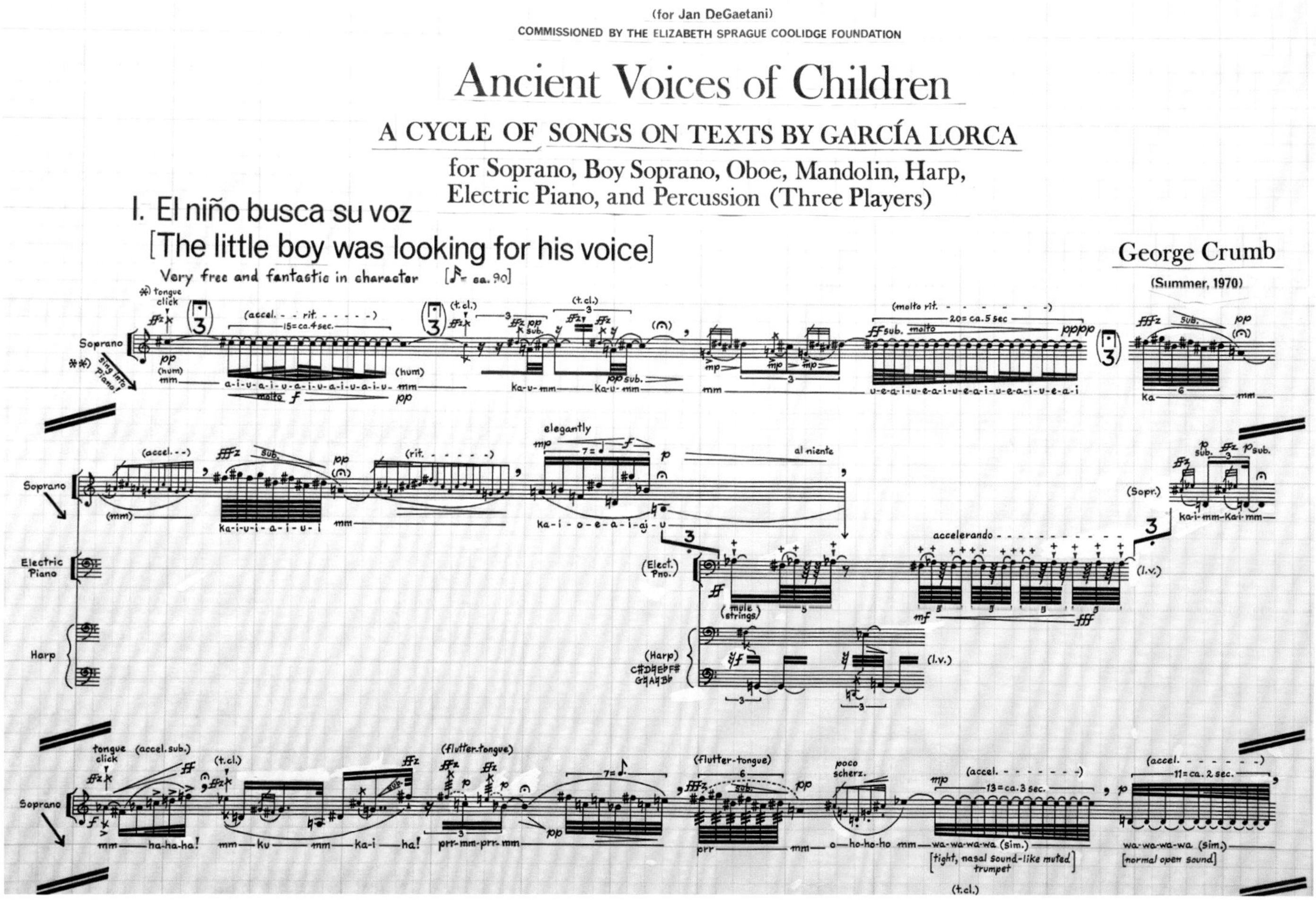

| Detail from holograph first page of George Crumb's *Ancient Voices of Children.*

and guests can marvel at the visual beauty of his meticulously constructed scores.

Contemporary Music and Modern Classics

Dispersed among the now-famous works that received their premieres at the Library are lesser-known gems that speak to the richness of new music offered to the public. Many of these were commissioned by Coolidge or through other Library funds, with their manuscripts becoming part of the collection. One of the exciting things about presenting new music is that one does not know what to expect—a work might take off right away or fade into obscurity after a single performance, regardless of its inherent qualities. Tastes and times change, and preserving these forays into the unknown allows future artists and researchers to rediscover works that have been neglected for whatever reason. The ability of the Library of Congress to program new music for its free concerts, without having to rely on ticket sales, remains a decided advantage when presenting the works of living or lesser-known composers.

Throughout the concert series' history, many commissions and premieres were performed as part of concerts that mixed older music with newer fare, by groups such as the Juilliard String Quartet. Over time, the number of ensembles dedicated solely to new music had an increased presence at the Library, and these appearances allowed the Library to pursue a wider range of commissions for different forces, and expand its diverse offerings within the poly-stylistic realm of new music.

Recent partners in this quest have included Ensemble Dal Niente, Klangforum Wien, the JACK Quartet, the Del Sol Quartet, and many more. Some composers come with their own ensembles, like Meredith Monk and her Vocal Ensemble. Intriguingly, groups have mirrored earlier pairings of "established and new" by presenting canonic works of the twentieth century alongside music written near the time of performance. These pairings serve to celebrate the accomplishments of composers and performers of

| Meredith Monk, left, and Vocal Ensemble, performing in the Coolidge Auditorium, October 30, 2015.

twentieth-century and new music, both of which are underperformed in comparison with works from the nineteenth century and before. A good example of this can be seen with Ensemble intercontemporain's November 13, 2015, performance that included new works by Han Lash and Matthias Pintscher alongside some twentieth-century standards: Edgard Varèse's *Octandre* (composed in 1923) and the chamber concertos of György Ligeti and Alban Berg.

The Library's support of modern music also includes educational opportunities for experts and amateurs. For instance, the Library restored the Buchla 100 modular synthesizer (ca. 1963) once used by Morton Subotnick, a pioneer of electronic music. On December 5, 2024, Subotnick and the team that revitalized the vintage equipment demonstrated it before a packed audience.

The Jazz Age

Perhaps nothing has transformed the breadth of Concerts from the Library of Congress as much as the infusion of new financial support for jazz. The 2010s saw a renaissance in the Library's jazz offerings, funded almost entirely through generous donations from the Reva and David Logan Foundation and the Revada Foundation of the Logan Family. While there were significant one-off jazz concerts in the 2000s featuring artists such as Paquito D'Rivera, Regina Carter, and Dave Brubeck, it was the steady support of the Logan family that allowed jazz programming to blossom. The success of that programming led to the first permanent fund at the Library that supports jazz specifically: the William I. Bandas Trust Fund, established in 2024.

The first strains of jazz played at the Library came from Nathaniel Shilkret and his chamber orchestra on Tuesday, October 8, 1929. The concert included songs collected and sung by John J. Niles with Marion Kirby (*Negro Exaltations* and *Kentucky Mountain Songs*). Other highlights included Werner Janssen's *Obsequies of a Saxophone; or, The American Mercury*, and an arrangement of W.C. Handy's *The St. Louis Blues*.

Mark Milanovich demonstrating how the Buchla 100 works in the Library of Congress flute vault, 2024. Morton Subotnick's Buchla 100 was built by Don Buchla and used in the wildly successful *Silver Apples of the Moon* (1967), the first electronic music album commissioned by a record label (Nonesuch). The analog Buchla 100 gave composers precise control over electronic sounds in a way not previously possible.

Top: Detail from the souvenir program for Jazz '96. From left: Buddy Collette, Gerald Wilson, and Benny Carter, all of whom led their orchestras in a three-day bash at the Lincoln Theater.

Bottom: The Mingus Quintet performed in The Arlene and Robert Kogod Cradle Theater at Arena Stage on April 14, 2023, as part of the Library's offsite offerings that season.

Composed in 1914, within fifteen years *The St. Louis Blues* had been recorded by Fats Waller, Bessie Smith, Louis Armstrong, and W.C. Handy himself.

The Library continued to periodically present jazz-inflected concerts, such as the June 3, 1962, Concert of Chamber Music Illustrating the Influence of Jazz. During the 1990s, jazz started to appear more regularly as part of the Library's offsite musical offerings while the Coolidge Auditorium was closed for renovation (1990–97). An especially memorable jazz event featured the Mingus Big Band, which performed on June 4, 1993, at the National Academy of Sciences. The ensemble used Mingus' own "lion head" bass for the concert, which marked the Library's acquisition of the Charles Mingus collection. As Jon Newsom, chief of the Music Division stated at the time, "This is the greatest, most important body of work related to a jazz composer that we've acquired."

One of the most exciting events of the 1990s was the Jazz '96 festival (June 6–8) at the Lincoln Theater in Washington, DC. The festival featured three large-scale concerts and three newly commissioned works from the headliners (funded by the Ira and Leonore Gershwin Fund): The Buddy Collette Big Band (*Friendships Suite: Sixty Years of Musical Togetherness*), The Gerald Wilson Orchestra (*Summertime*, an adaptation of music from *Porgy and Bess*), and The Benny Carter Orchestra (*Peaceful Warrior*). All of these bandleaders were at the top

Right: Senior Music Specialist Larry Appelbaum speaks at an event celebrating the centennial of Ella Fitzgerald in the Whittall Pavilion, April 25, 2017.

Below: Cecil Taylor in performance on February 12, 1999. That concert featured the premiere of Algonquin, commissioned by the McKim Fund in the Library of Congress, performed with violinist Mat Maneri. The recording of the live performance was released in 2004 by Bridge Records in their Great Performances from the Library of Congress series.

of their profession, with two (Wilson and Carter) being recognized by the National Endowment for the Arts as "Jazz Masters," and the public flocked to this extraordinary big band summit. A few years later Cecil Taylor, one of the great jazz pianists, gave a concert in the newly renovated Coolidge Auditorium.

A wide generational range of performers have been presented at the Library, from seasoned artists such as McCoy Tyner and Abdullah Ibrahim, to midcareer musicians such as Cécile McLorin Salvant and Aaron Diehl, in addition to rising stars like Jazzmeia Horn and Lakecia Benjamin. Latin jazz artists also figured prominently in the 2010s and 2020s, including Chucho Valdés, Gonzalo Rubalcaba, Aymée Nuviola, and Eddie Palmieri, performing to enthusiastic crowds. With the Library's ever-increasing volume of jazz collections, visiting jazz artists have been able to connect with the Library's holdings just as classical musicians have. Seeing direct ties to important figures and music through correspondence, photographs, copyright deposits, and manuscripts helps people to value and appreciate their own contributions to music in a new light.

In the 2010s, with the help of philanthropists Dan and Gloria Logan, the Library of Congress Jazz Scholars program began. Under its auspices, the Library has presented talks and writings by scholars and artists such as Terri Lyne Carrington, Ingrid Monson,

Opposite page, top: Pianist, composer, and bandleader Chucho Valdés holding a picture of himself with Max Roach, taken in Cuba in the 1980s, and held in the Library's Max Roach Collection in the Music Division.

Opposite page, bottom: Pianist and composer Gonzalo Rubalcaba and singer Aymée Nuviola looking at a manuscript in the Gershwin Room at the Library of Congress.

This page, below: Billy Strayhorn, New York, ca. 1946–48.

Right: Billy Strayhorn, "Take the 'A' Train," 1939, holograph manuscript.

Dan Morgenstern, and Robert O'Meally. The Revada Foundation also supported special projects, such as the Salute to Strayhorn, a multiday affair from June 8 to 10, 2023, that included the Bill Charlap Trio with Jon Faddis, a Big Band evening with Loren Schoenberg and Russell Malone, several films incorporating Billy Strayhorn's music, a symposium, and a lecture by Strayhorn biographer David Hajdu. These events marked the arrival of the Strayhorn Collection at the Library. Although recognized for his compositions "Take the 'A' Train" and "Lush Life," Strayhorn historically has remained in the shadow of his longtime collaborator, Duke Ellington. The Library's festival celebrated the musician's considerable achievements, known and unknown.

Another celebration took place in November 2024 to mark the centennial of Max Roach, whose papers are also held at the Library. Composer Tyshawn Sorey, whose music seems to transcend genre, composed a new work inspired by Roach for the Tyshawn Sorey Trio and Sandbox Percussion. Almost exactly twenty-five years before this concert, on November 13, 1999, Max Roach himself performed at the Library with the Beijing Trio, with Jon Jang at the piano and Jiebing Chen playing erhu. Roach's family celebrated the posthumous arrival of his collection at the Library in 2014.

Opposite page: The Beijing Trio with Max Roach on drums during a performance at the Library of Congress on November 13, 1999.

Below: An excerpt from the "Freedom Day" movement of Max Roach's Freedom Now Suite (1960).

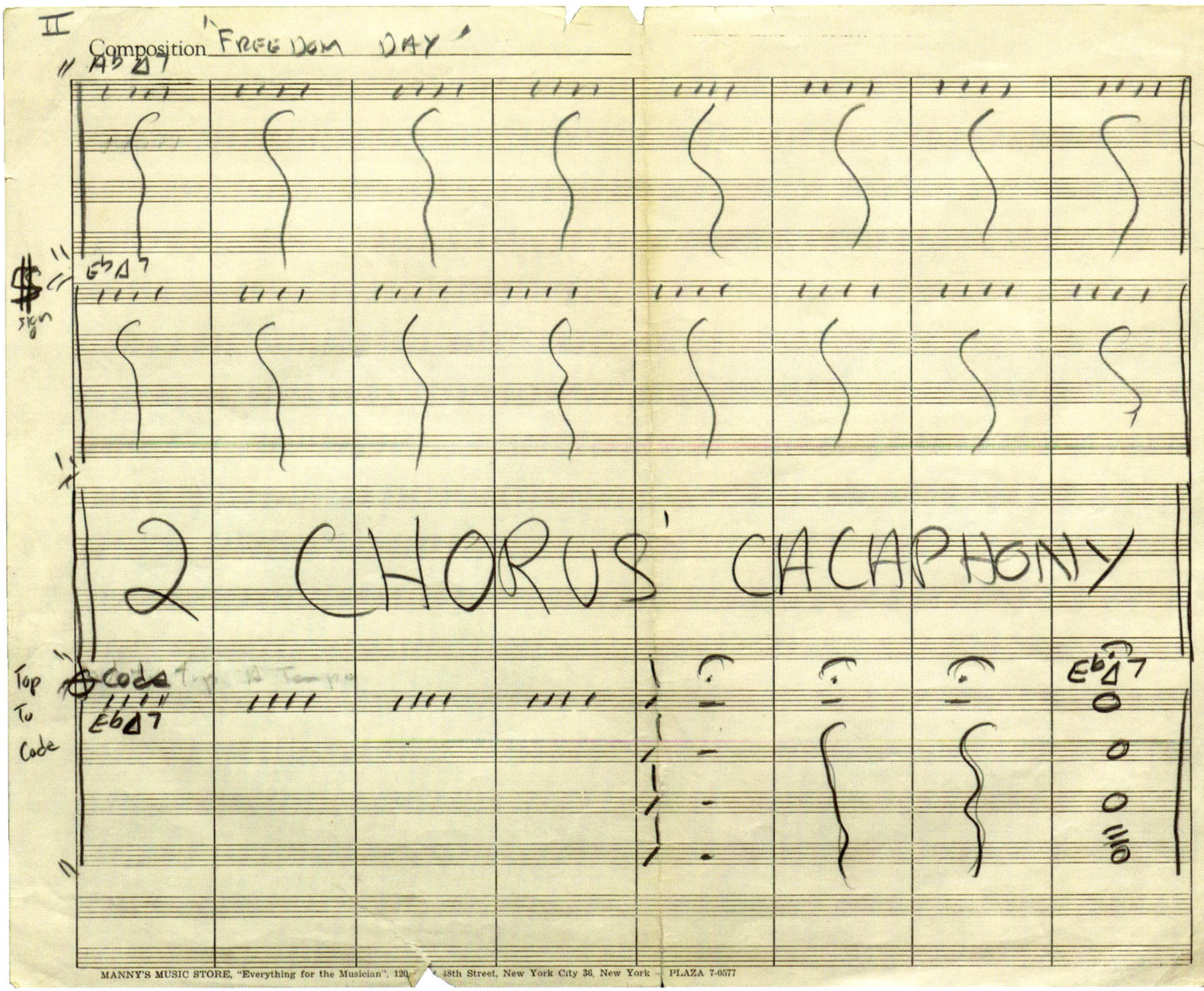

UNIVERSITE
EST.
1889

Scene 3: Bringing the Collections to Life

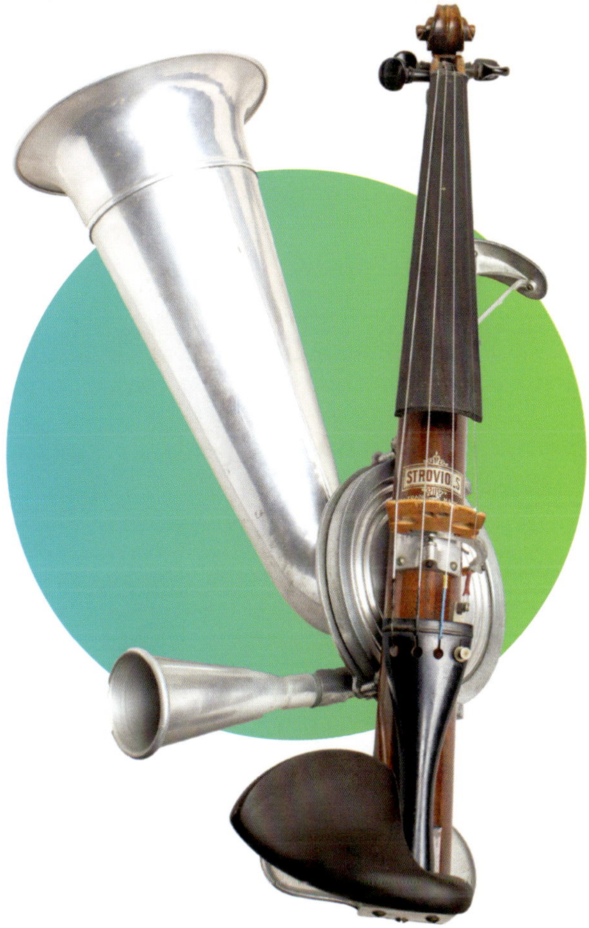

If there were a watchword for the development of Concerts from the Library of Congress, it might be *augmentation*. The sense of exploration is palpable, yet preservation of the roots and identity of the series as a bastion of classical chamber music remained critical to its mission. Tradition and innovation joined forces to give the public new content and unprecedented access to the Library's collections.

The Concerts from the Library of Congress series brings the Library's collections to life in myriad ways: giving voice to its instruments, invigorating unheard content from the stacks, using its treasures to engender new ones, and so on. In time, the nature of the series has expanded, animating the Coolidge Auditorium and other venues with special presentations. When confronted with closures, Concerts from the Library of Congress found innovative ways to maintain its core mission of serving the public and illuminating the Library's collections.

Museums and libraries that collect functional instruments have a challenging task: to accommodate the principal purpose of an instrument—an artifact whose artistic value is tied to its sound—in performance, and at the same time to preserve it for posterity. The Library of Congress successfully manages this balancing act for many of its most important instrumental holdings, making them available for playing and for valuable research projects to enhance and share knowledge.

Following the deaths of Elizabeth Sprague Coolidge (1953) and Serge Koussevitzky (1951)—the two primary outside forces for new music patronage at the Library during the early years of the series—the Music Division chiefs remained committed to commissioning and presenting new music, absorbing their work into the Library's own collections and commissioning endeavors. What makes the Library unique among commissioning entities is that all of the holograph manuscripts (that is, music written in the composer's hand)—or their modern-day prepublication equivalent in a signed, computer-produced version—are added to the Library's collection for preservation. In addition, almost all events produced at the Library of Congress have been documented and are themselves an important part of the Library's collections.

The vast scope of materials in the Music Division—the largest such collection in the world—means that the holdings are fertile ground for exploration and discovery. Collection-centric programming serves to enrich the public's

Opposite page: Students from Howard University's Chadwick A. Boseman College of Fine Arts view musical theater collections along with Dean Phylicia Rashad, November 7, 2023.

Above: Stroh Violin, gift of George D. Powell, 1994. Invented by John Mathias Stroh and built around 1904, the Strohviol was an early solution for the difficulties in recording string instruments. The large horn would be directed toward the recording apparatus, and the smaller horn would be used in the player's ear like a modern-day monitor. Like the concert series, the Stroh violin sat at the intersection of tradition and innovation.

understanding of and access to the resources preserved at the Library. In addition to offering compelling programming from world-class artists, the Library augments the experience with displays, preconcert conversations, lectures, and commentary whenever possible. This commitment to context gives audiences the opportunity to gain insight into the creative process and to interact with historical documents and unique collections that help bring the past to life.

Instruments on Loan

While the quintet of Whittall Stradivari instruments stays almost exclusively at the Library, other instruments in the Library's portfolio can go out into the world. For instance, a violin (ca. 1870–71) and bow by Jean-Baptiste Vuillaume, donated in 2000 by Mildred B. French, widow of violinist James Corbett French, has been loaned to musicians including Nurit Bar-Josef, the concertmaster of the National Symphony Orchestra. An instrument that has seen a lot of performances in the Coolidge Auditorium and beyond is the "Fulton, ex Baird, Tuscan-Medici" viola built by Antonio Stradivari in 1690 in Cremona. This remarkable viola—one of only a dozen or so Stradivari violas left in the world—had been on loan to the Library of Congress from 1977 to 2025 courtesy of The Tuscan Corporation and the family of Cameron Baird. It was acquired for the Library permanently in 2025 through the generosity of the David and Amy Fulton Foundation, The Tuscan Corporation, and the Baird family. The list of musicians who have played this instrument in recital or as part of a chamber group reads as a "who's who" of modern viola royalty: Kikuei Ikeda, Kim Kashkashian, and Richard O'Neill, among many others. The "Fulton, ex Baird, Tuscan-Medici" can travel for performances offsite and can often be heard in the hands of Roberto Díaz, president of the Curtis Institute of Music.

The "Goldberg Baron Vitta" violin built by Giuseppe Guarneri del Gesù (ca. 1730) is a "twin" to the incredible "Kreisler" Guarneri del Gesù given to the Library by Fritz Kreisler in 1952. The "Goldberg Baron Vitta," formerly owned by Szymon Goldberg, was donated to the Library in 2006. Since then, it has been played by Nicholas Kitchen of the Borromeo String Quartet.

Top: The "Fulton, ex-Baird, Tuscan-Medici" viola by Antonio Stradivari, in the ceremonial office of the Librarian of Congress on March 11, 2025, the date ownership was fully transferred to the Library of Congress.

Bottom: Violin by Giuseppe Guarneri, Cremona, ca. 1730, known as the "Kreisler." The "Kreisler" has been used in performance at the Library by artists ranging from Curtis Stewart to Anne-Sophie Mutter.

Playing the Library's Violins

by Nicholas Kitchen, Violinist, Borromeo String Quartet

Nicholas Kitchen performing Bach's *Chaconne* from the second partita for solo violin, BWV 1004, on the Kreisler Guarneri del Gesú, 2007. Kitchen recorded the *Chaconne* using five of the Library's instruments and used a technique called "simulscore" to allow the viewer to follow's Bach's handwritten manuscript of the piece for each performance.

I feel incredibly fortunate to have had extensive personal experience playing on the violins in the collection of the Library of Congress. This has happened in three arenas. The first is my ongoing use of the "Goldberg Baron Vitta" Guarneri del Gesù in most of my performances since 2006. This was the violin of my teacher, the distinguished soloist, chamber musician, and conductor Szymon Goldberg. The violin was given to the Library of Congress by Goldberg's widow, the pianist and educator Miyoko Yamane Goldberg, and it was given with the condition that I use it during my career and help to determine a future artist to use the violin that would play and teach in ways celebrating the special beauty and integrity that were part of Szymon Goldberg's artistry. This violin has a fantastic purity of tone and a kind of fieriness in its presence. I feel so fortunate to bring the sound of this violin into quartet concerts and solo concerts all around the world. So this violin's exciting voice has been brought by me to playing all the Beethoven quartets, all the Bartók quartets, Mozart, Haydn, Brahms—the list goes on in the most wonderful way!

The two other arenas for exploring the instruments of the Library of Congress are events that happened within the Library. In one of them, I played the six sonatas and partitas for solo violin by J. S. Bach (BWV 1001–06) in a single concert in the Coolidge Auditorium. The concert celebrated multiple layers of master craftsmanship from the early 1700s. There was the music itself, but while I played the music, every page of Bach's beautiful manuscripts of these works was projected for the audience to see. For this performance I used five of the treasured violins in the Library's collection. I also explained in between the performances my own view of the interwoven features of these six compositions. On the stage were five violins carefully arrayed on a table, and I played the sonata no. 1 in G minor on the Goldberg Guarneri; Partita no. 1 in B minor on the Castelbarco Stradivarius; sonata no. 2 in A minor on the Betts Stradivarius; Partita no. 2 in D minor on the Brookings Amati; sonata no. 3 in C major on the Kreisler Guarneri del Gesù; and Partita no. 3 in E major on the Goldberg Guarneri again. I had chosen each violin with the intention of matching its particular character of tone to the piece. The intensity and clarity of the Goldberg matched with the intensity of the Sonata no. 1 and the brightness of the Partita no. 3. The Castelbarco with its luminous transparency matched the Partita no. 1; the Betts with its palpable strength made it a great musical platform for the Sonata no. 2. The darkness of the Brookings Amati was perfect for the Partita no. 2 and the grandeur of the river of sound made by the Kreisler Guarneri was perfect for the grandeur of the sonata no. 3. I could not have felt more fortunate than to delve into the rich combination of the greatest music played on the greatest instruments!

The third arena was the Borromeo Quartet playing the Stradivari celebration concert. The Borromeo has played more than one, but the most memorable was when we performed all six Bartók string quartets in one concert. There was a preconcert element that also delved into the content of the manuscripts of these pieces, and then we had the rare privilege of having all four players working with these peerless tools. The complexity of what this combination of qualities does to sound is hard to explain in a few words, but in this case the audience was able to revel in this sound for three hours. And all of us could celebrate how one of these quartets, String Quartet no. 5, was in fact brought into being through the generous commissioning of Elizabeth Sprague Coolidge. In all of these things, I feel tremendous gratitude for what the instrument makers have given us, what the composers have given us, and what the Library of Congress gives all of us by bringing all these elements together so that we are all able to share music in the best possible way. ■

The World's Largest Collection of Flutes

Although they are not frequently played in concerts, the Library's collection of flutes—the largest individual collection of instruments at the Library—has been important beyond the concert sphere, inspiring lectures, symposia, and conferences. The extensive Dayton C. Miller collection comprises 1,700 flutes and other wind instruments, iconography, and flute-centric books and music. It is among the largest such collections in the world.

Miller donated his expansive collection of flutes, other wind instruments, iconography, manuscripts, sculptures, and more to the Library in 1941. Other instruments have been added to the collection over the years by various donors. The collection has been the subject of several research projects that have been featured in concert series events. One intriguing example was the study undertaken of the Laurent glass and crystal flutes with a grant from the National Endowment for the Humanities aimed at identifying preservation vulnerabilities in the glass objects. Special panel discussions and lecture-performances have developed from work done with the collection, including the "Two Thousand Flutes" lecture-recital with flutist Lorna McGhee, pianist Ryo Yanagitani and the Library's musical instrument curator Carol Lynn Ward Bamford offered in 2015.

The concert series has seen its share of excellent commissions for winds. For instance, the New York Woodwind Quintet appeared with pianist Rosalyn Tureck on February 19, 1954, when they premiered the Concerto for Piano and Woodwind Quintet, op. 53, by Wallingford Riegger, commissioned by the Koussevitzky Foundation. Jean-Pierre Rampal performed the flute sonata by Francis Poulenc (a Coolidge commission) at the Library on February 14, 1958. In more recent times, Windsync premiered a newly commissioned work by Paul Lansky (*The Long and Short of It*) on October 24, 2015.

Top: Dayton C. Miller with flute, undated. Miller was an amateur flutist, flute maker, flute collector, and vocationally a scientist who had a fifty-year career teaching at Case School of Applied Science (Case Western Reserve University), where he ultimately led the physics department. He was a deeply curious individual who pioneered the use of x-rays; he also invented a device that could transfer sound waves into a visual image, anticipating myriad uses for that technology in the computer age. His expertise in acoustics was such that he was consulted on the potential acoustic properties of the Coolidge Auditorium when it was built in 1925.

Middle: Lizzo brought international attention to the glass flutes in the collection on September 26, 2022, when the pop phenomenon performed with the crystal flute once owned by President James Madison. Instrument maker Claude Laurent gave the flute to Madison in 1813, and it was purportedly rescued from the White House the following year after the British set the building aflame.

Bottom: Pianist Solungga Liu in performance at the Library of Congress, November 4, 2017. Liu premiered Charles Tomlinson Griffes's transcription of *Les parfums de la nuit* from the *Ibéria* section of Debussy's *Images* for orchestra.

From Shelf to Sound

The Library's instruments have provided ample inspiration for programming, but the holdings in general—the largest such collection in the world—are a vital source of content. Some concerts have explored lesser-known composers, such as Charles Tomlinson Griffes, a talented American composer and pianist who died in 1920 at the age of thirty-five. The Library holds a number of his works in manuscript, and his music has been featured periodically, as in the September 21, 1984, Concerts from the Collections: On the 100th Anniversary of the Birth of Charles Tomlinson Griffes, with soprano Phyllis Bryn-Julson and pianist James Tocco. In November 2017 pianist Solungga Liu featured Griffes's piano music in a "Griffes Rediscovered" program; in addition to a preconcert lecture contextualizing Griffes's work, this event featured what is believed to be the premiere of a Griffes transcription of music by Debussy, drawn from a manuscript in the collection.

In some cases, concerts have illuminated lesser-known aspects of a familiar figure. Pianist Artur Schnabel, for example—known for his advocacy and performance of Beethoven's music—was revealed to have a modernist streak in a performance on November 30, 2018, by pianist Jenny Lin, soprano Marlissa Hudson, and violinist Cornelius Dufallo. The concert featured some of Schnabel's own forward-looking compositions alongside his earlier Romantic-leaning works and Lieder by Brahms. This event was paired with a screening of the film *Artur Schnabel: No Place of Exile* (2017) in the Library's Mary Pickford Theater. The film, directed by Matthew Mishory, explores the travels of Schnabel after fleeing Berlin in 1933 and uses his compositions—some held in the Library's collection—to offer a new perspective on the great Beethoven interpreter.

Stacked with Inspiration

In addition to the resuscitation of lesser-known scores in the collection, Concerts from the Library of Congress has explored the transformation of existing works through performances drawing on new editions, transcriptions for other instrumental forces, or presentation in a new guise (such as pairing existing music with dance). A particularly memorable example occurred at the close of the 2023–24 season, with Charles Martin Loeffler's Octet.

Loeffler had once been considered a major American composer, but

Left: Artur Schnabel at the piano, ca. 1920–25.

Below: Schnabel, page one of *Klavierstück 1937*, holograph manuscript. The Library's collection also includes extensive editorial annotations Schnabel prepared for his edition of the Beethoven piano sonatas.

Charles Martin Loeffler, Octet, page 1, 1896–7, holograph manuscript. The path from the manuscript to a viable score and parts is one filled with editorial decisions that require care in the absence of the composer's presence. Manuscripts also provide insight into the original ideas that the composer had, such as the crossed-out notes on the first page of Loeffler's octet.

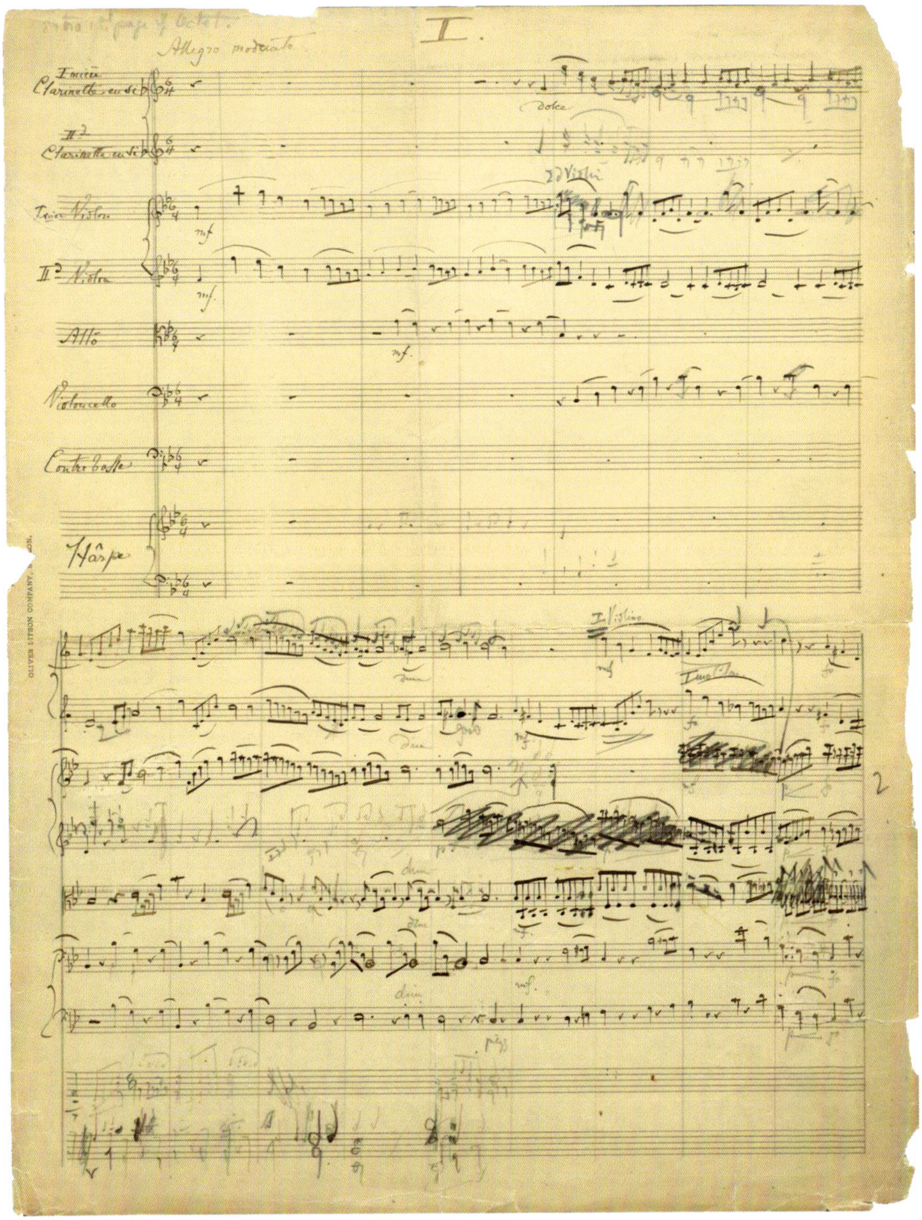

time and lack of advocacy let his music fall into obscurity. Loeffler's Octet from 1897 is not believed to have had more than a pair of performances in the year it was composed; it then stayed silent on the Library's shelves, as Loeffler did not pursue publication. In the early 2020s clarinetist Graeme Steele Johnson began exploring this work, orchestrated for two clarinets, harp, string quartet, and contrabass. Johnson reconciled the Library's manuscript score and parts to create an edition that could be played by a top-tier ensemble he put together. After 120-plus years without a performance, Johnson's group took the piece on tour, including a poignant reunification of the performed music with Loeffler's manuscript at the Library on May 22, 2024. The event included an in-depth discussion of the editorial process with Music Division staff.

At the close of that same season, a fascinating project led to the development of new chamber music based on existing sources. This project involved the music of composer Irving Fine, whose chamber music output was limited by his untimely death at the age of 47 and whose papers are held by the Library. In addition to his string quartet, Fine wrote two wind quintets that are seminal works in the literature. In 2024, that body of work was augmented when the Zéphyros Winds performed a new transcription of Fine's *Diversions* (1959–60). Originally composed in two versions—one for piano and one for orchestra—a new wind quintet transcription was created by composer Jeff Scott, former horn player of the Imani Winds. Paired with a performance of the original piano version by Audrey Andrist, it offered an opportunity to hear Fine's music reimagined, courtesy of the Verna and Irving Fine Endowment in the Library of Congress.

As one of the world's most important repositories for the music of Franz Liszt, the Library was the perfect site to program an event that combined the elements of reconstruction and transcription described above. On April 27, 2019, audiences were treated to a rarity in opera: a newly reconstructed work by a major composer. David Trippett gave a lecture on Liszt's unfinished opera *Sardanapalo* and collaborated with singers from the Domingo-Cafritz Young Artists Program of the Washington National Opera, offering a sense of what an Italian opera by Liszt might have sounded like had he finished the project, begun in 1845 but abandoned in 1852. Trippett edited and reconstructed a piano-vocal score and a full orchestral version of the opera's only completed act. The work, performed at the Library in the version for piano and voices, has the hallmarks of Lisztian composition but draws on the Italian operatic tradition of composers such as Vincenzo Bellini, whose work Liszt paraphrased in compositions for the piano.

Franz Liszt, *Réminiscences de Norma de Bellini*, first edition, 1843, p. 20. Liszt composed many paraphrases and fantasies on operatic themes for solo piano, engaging with popular Italian operas in particular. This example shows the climactic section from Liszt's "remembrance" of Vincenzo Bellini's opera *Norma*, exhibiting Liszt's grasp of Italian drama. Operas by composers such as Bellini likely influenced the composition of Liszt's *Sardanapalo*.

Hedging our Betts: "Antonius Stradivarius Oberlinensis"

by Carol Lynn Ward-Bamford, Curator of Musical Instruments, Music Division

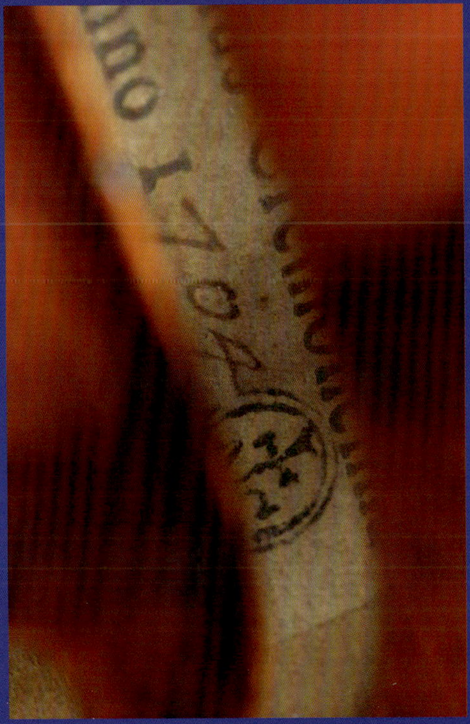

Detail with construction year for the famed "Betts" violin of by Antonio Stradivari, Cremona, 1704. The label is located inside the instrument.

The Library's instruments are living artifacts, worthy of study and emulation beyond their uses in performance. A wonderful example of art bred by art, an incredible melding of technologies led to the creation of the "Oberlin Betts," one of the more recent instruments to enter the Library's collection. Of the three violins given to the Library by Gertrude Clarke Whittall, the Betts Stradivari, made in 1704, has long had the reputation of being one of the most copied violins by Stradivari. Admired and revered by luthiers for its beauty, its perfection, and remarkable state of preservation, the Betts has also been sought after by the world's leading violinists and audiences for its sound. After all, it was made by the sixty-year-old master at the golden prime of his genius.

Well before the advent of innovative technologies such as the 3D printer, the iconic Betts violin was copied by violinmakers and amateurs eager to replicate its f-holes, long corners and archings, the woods Stradivari used, and, of course, his varnish. Early copies were made without violin makers ever seeing the Betts in person. Estimates of size were passed along by word of mouth or written description from a magazine or book. Two-dimensional images, such as black and white photographs, color photographs, and posters, provided a visual guide for making a replica. When the Whittall Stradivari instruments arrived at the Library in 1935, the Betts violin was finally and permanently available for all to see in person, for makers to copy by tracing the violin's outline on a piece of paper with a pencil, and for audiences to hear via the Library's radio broadcasts, recordings, and live concerts.

The process changed in 2011, more than three-hundred years after the Betts was created, when a copy was made at the Oberlin Violinmaker's Workshop, a collaborative summer program in Ohio for professionals to study, document, and advance knowledge about important stringed instruments. The Antonius Stradivarius Oberlinensis / Faciebat Anno 2011, as the printed label inside reads, was built from a CT (computed tomography) scan, a CNC (computer numerical controlled) machine, and the hands of fifty-eight of the world's top luthiers. Their signatures are handwritten inside the violin.

When the Betts violin was taken to Oberlin—a rare excursion from the Library—practitioners could see, hear, and discover in great technical detail the facts behind Stradivari's technique such as the density, dimensions, thickness, and structure of the woods he chose. In return, the workshop generated new technical reference documents for researchers to study. The Oberlin violinmakers went back to their benches and classes to teach a new generation of aspiring luthiers what they had seen, learned, and made.

The digital files of the 3D object were shared and saved, and a replica created with a greater degree of accuracy than ever before. Future copies of the Betts can be made again and again and, through experimentation and manipulation of the data, other instruments such as a viola can be created. As a result, the Betts remains one the most copied Stradivari instruments and, at least to the trained eye, now one of the most instantly recognizable Stradivari violins.

The Oberlin copy was completed in 2012 and, like the original, was a masterpiece. It was purchased and donated to the Music Division in 2013, thanks to the generosity of Dr. William Sloan and Professor Judy Sloan. And, in a double world premiere at the Library, Gregory Walker debuted the Oberlin Betts in a concert that also introduced *Bleu*, for unaccompanied violin, composed by his father George Walker. Dr. Sloan, who had a hand in making the Betts copy, remarked that as a young violinist and medical resident he had visited the Whittall Stradivari Collection. Accompanied by Professor Sloan on piano, Dr. Sloan decided during the performance not only to learn more about stringed instruments but also to make and collect them.

Access to an instrument, through exhibit, examination, and performance is inspiring. Whittall's bequest insisted that the Stradivari instruments not remain locked forever within an exhibit case. Consequently, her gift opened the door to expanded opportunities for makers, musicians, students, and audiences to see the Betts, to hear the Betts, and to study and to copy the Betts in new ways, creating a new vocabulary and understanding of the 1704 Betts Stradivari and the 2011 Oberlin Betts. ■

Inside rib of the 2011 Oberlin Betts, with luthiers' signatures and label.

Content in Context

Coolidge's original vision for the concert series included support for the study of music. Lectures, panels, symposia, and educational workshops have been a hallmark of the series since 1925. Talks often featured contemporary scholarship resulting in part from research in the Performing Arts Reading Room, lectures by visiting composers and scholars, and preconcert talks with performers and curators. The Library continues this practice in the twenty-first century, while also developing new and varied methods to contextualize its programs and engage the public through new technologies and interactive events.

Speakers are often renowned figures in their fields. For instance, a symposium in 1930 included a lecture by David Mannes (who had founded the Mannes School of Music in New York City in 1916) on "Music in the Museum." In 1932 the audience was treated to the first of several addresses by composer Gustav Holst (of *The Planets* fame), who spoke at a concert celebrating Joseph Haydn's bicentenary. In 1945 the Louis C. Elson Fund was created, which has allowed Library reading rooms to host lectures by major scholarly figures, from Jacques Barzun and H. C. Robbins Landon to Helen Hartness Flanders and Charles Rosen, among many others.

Since 2008 the Library has maintained an annual series of lectures given by members of the American Musicological Society whose research was in part conducted using the Music Division's collections. The series has featured many modern scholars of note, beginning with Judith Tick's lecture, "Ruth Crawford Seeger, Modernist Composer in the Folk Revival: Biography and Music History." Other major scholars and writers have lectured as part of thematically linked celebrations, like the bicentennial celebration of Richard Wagner's birth. Programming that season included Alex Ross on "Wagner in America" (November 23, 2013) and Liszt/Chopin biographer Alan Walker—who has presented numerous lectures at the Library—offering a talk "In Defense of Transcription" (November 9, 2013). Lectures, book talks, and interviews about independent topics allow the Library to address areas of music that cannot easily be explored on the Coolidge stage, such as music calibrated for performance in a stadium, or music for a specific cultural context, as with some African ceremonial music. Some featured speakers in this vein have included Graham Nash, Kofi Agawu, Stew, and Hisham Aidi, to name just a few. Topics have ranged from Cold War hip hop to pop figures and the record industry.

In time, the Library developed other ways of serving the collections. Between 2009 and 2011, the Library presented *Music and the Brain*, a groundbreaking, interdisciplinary series of lectures on the neuroscience of music. The lectures were later released as a podcast series, earning the most streams of any Library of Congress podcast. The Music and the Brain podcast series features leading scholars and artists, ranging from composer Tod Machover, surgeon and neuroscientist Dr. Charles Limb, and clinical psychologist and writer Kay Redfield Jamison (*An Unquiet Mind*, 1995, and *Robert Lowell, Setting the River on Fire*, 2017, which was a finalist for the Pulitzer Prize for Biography) to bestselling author, psychologist, and neuroscientist Dr. Daniel Levitin (*This is Your Brain on Music*, 2006).

Music Division staff also developed targeted "#Declassified" briefings open to the public that offered curated, detailed access to special collections. There also have been film series—among the most popular have been the various jazz film series prepared by the Library's jazz expert Larry Appelbaum, primarily taking place in the Library's Mary Pickford Theater, as well as curated topical offerings (using when possible the Library's carefully preserved 35mm prints), with ties to the Library's special collections, as in the sample survey of Erich Korngold's film music in 2019.

Interactive adventures have also been explored as part of the concert series. From augmented reality (ZOFO piano duo, 2020) to an interactive composition inspired by video game music, the Library consistently seeks new ways to enhance its offerings. The interactive composition *Arrows* (2019) by Austin Wintory was part of a larger festival about the history and practice of video game music.

Quatuor van Kuijk performing in the Great Hall of the Library of Congress on February 8, 2023.

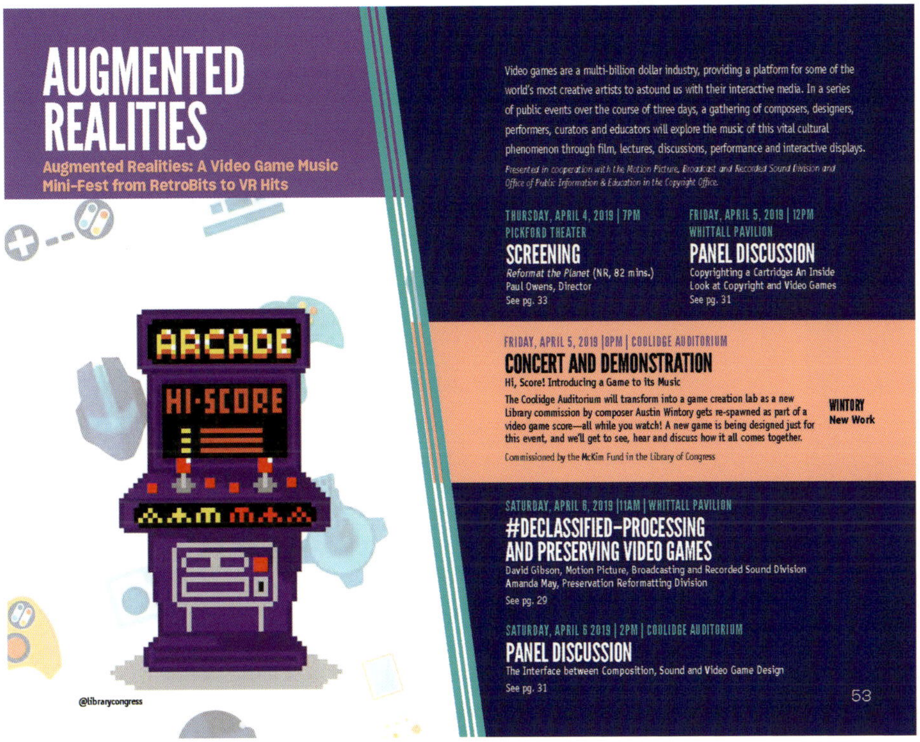
AUGMENTED REALITIES

Augmented Realities: A Video Game Music Mini-Fest from RetroBits to VR Hits

ARCADE

HI-SCORE

@librarycongress

Video games are a multi-billion dollar industry, providing a platform for some of the world's most creative artists to astound us with their interactive media. In a series of public events over the course of three days, a gathering of composers, designers, performers, curators and educators will explore the music of this vital cultural phenomenon through film, lectures, discussions, performance and interactive displays.

Presented in cooperation with the Motion Picture, Broadcast and Recorded Sound Division and Office of Public Information & Education in the Copyright Office.

THURSDAY, APRIL 4, 2019 | 7PM
PICKFORD THEATER
SCREENING
Reformat the Planet (NR, 82 mins.)
Paul Owens, Director
See pg. 33

FRIDAY, APRIL 5, 2019 | 12PM
WHITTALL PAVILION
PANEL DISCUSSION
Copyrighting a Cartridge: An Inside Look at Copyright and Video Games
See pg. 31

FRIDAY, APRIL 5, 2019 |8PM | COOLIDGE AUDITORIUM
CONCERT AND DEMONSTRATION
Hi, Score! Introducing a Game to its Music
The Coolidge Auditorium will transform into a game creation lab as a new Library commission by composer Austin Wintory gets re-spawned as part of a video game score—all while you watch! A new game is being designed just for this event, and we'll get to see, hear and discuss how it all comes together.
WINTORY
New Work
Commissioned by the McKim Fund in the Library of Congress

SATURDAY, APRIL 6, 2019 |11AM | WHITTALL PAVILION
#DECLASSIFIED–PROCESSING AND PRESERVING VIDEO GAMES
David Gibson, Motion Picture, Broadcasting and Recorded Sound Division
Amanda May, Preservation Reformatting Division
See pg. 29

SATURDAY, APRIL 6 2019 | 2PM | COOLIDGE AUDITORIUM
PANEL DISCUSSION
The Interface between Composition, Sound and Video Game Design
See pg. 31

53

Left: "Augmented Realities" brochure listing for a video game festival, 2019. In addition to an interactive commission, the festival included an arcade featuring an assortment of video games, from vintage to virtual reality, that the public could play. Attendees could then experience a history of video game music as it was intended to be encountered—in the game. Winnifred Phillips, who gave a talk at the Library about "The Interface Between Music Composition and Game Design," was the 2025 recipient of a Grammy award in the Best Score Soundtrack for Videogames and Other Interactive Media category, a category established in 2022.

Right: Performance of Roger Reynolds's *JUSTICE* (1999) in the Great Hall of the Library of Congress, November 30, 2001. Performed by soprano Carmen Pelton, actor Donnah Welby and percussionist Steven Schick, supported by sound and computer engineers Peter Otto, Josef Kucera, and Ralph Pitt from the University of California at San Diego. All three performers portrayed aspects of Clytemnestra's character in this adaptation of the story of Clytemnestra, Agamemnon, and Iphigenia from Aeschylus and Euripides.

Letting the People Hear It Outside of the Coolidge Auditorium

On numerous occasions other venues have been a part of the concert series, with thrilling results. Performances have taken place in the Whittall Pavilion, the Great Hall of the Thomas Jefferson Building, individual reading rooms, and around Washington, DC, including at the Atlas Performing Arts Center, the Hill Center, Arena Stage, the Lincoln Theater, and the Academy of Sciences. Under the right circumstances, a change of venue can be more appropriate for the music or to allow audiences to experience and interact with it in different ways.

A key location for music performances outside of the Coolidge Auditorium is the marbled Great Hall. This is a tricky space for music due to its extremely live acoustics, which can be positive for fullness of sound but difficult for clarity. Certain events have capitalized on the majesty of the space to great effect. The bicentennial anniversary of the Library of Congress in 2000 was also the centennial of the birth of Aaron Copland, whose collection is one of the mainstays of the Library's American music holdings. The concert series had a special celebration that featured the Orpheus Chamber Orchestra and music from The Copland House, which was showcased in National Public Radio broadcasts.

Left: One of three proposed configurations for the renovated Coolidge Auditorium. Physical model by George Izenour. This model was not implemented precisely this way during the 1990s Coolidge renovation, but it shows one of the creative acoustic paneling proposals Izenour had for a modular design that retained the Coolidge's principal features. **Middle/Right:** The Coolidge Auditorium with chairs removed and reinstalled during an August 1962 renovation that included the installation of an air conditioner. **Opposite page:** Violinist Jannina Norpoth of PUBLIQuartet performs *A Shared Solitary* by Niloufar Nourbakhsh for the Boccaccio Project. The performance was self-produced due to the COVID-19 pandemic. Released in June 2020.

On November 14, 2000, a new McKim commission by Roberto Sierra premiered as part of an all-Copland program given by the "The President's Own" United States Marine Band, pianist Michael Boriskin, and the Orpheus Chamber Orchestra. Copland's *Midday Thoughts* (1944/1982) was orchestrated for the occasion by composer David Del Tredici. Later in the festival, on November 18, the Great Hall felt the resounding peals of brass instruments with three fanfares commissioned for the centennial from David Diamond, Lukas Foss, and Tania León.

Other creative uses of the Great Hall followed, including its use for the premiere of Roger Reynolds's chamber opera *Justice* on November 30, 2001. This dramatic work based on Aeschylus and Euripides includes three performers and features multichannel computer sound with live electronic manipulation of the music. Reynolds's collection is held at the Library and the Library's website features extensive resources about the composer's work, including many interviews with him.

Pivoting for Closures

While it can be exhilarating to explore other venues by choice, it can be challenging when uncontrollable circumstances necessitate it. The most significant and trying times away from the Coolidge were during its modern remodel (1990–97), the height of the COVID-19 pandemic (when all programming went virtual), and the Christmas Eve flood of 2022, when a burst pipe dumped some 10,000 gallons of water into the auditorium, forcing a five-month closure of the hall. Each of these required deft responses from Library staff to make the most of the situation and still give the public access to great music.

The Coolidge Auditorium's closure in 1990 for much-needed renovations lasted far longer than initially planned, necessitating the

prolonged use of other venues around Washington, DC. The renovations, which upgraded the auditorium's facilities while preserving the remarkable acoustic environment, included the installation of a new technical gallery above the stage with appropriate electrical, recording, video, and communications links; new lighting systems and new stage rigging, including acoustical drapery assemblies; a new orchestra pit mechanism with a stage apron lift and seat wagon; and a new catwalk, backstage elevator, and retractable cinema screen.

However, it was the 2020 closure that provoked an existential crisis for all performance venues. The onset of the COVID-19 pandemic brought with it the realization that innovative solutions were needed for the concert series to continue. The Library swiftly pivoted to virtual performances, providing much-needed support for the artistic community while maintaining the continuity of the series.

The Library also moved quickly to develop and implement the Boccaccio Project, a micro-commissioning venture supported by the Dina Koston and Roger Shapiro Fund. In the mid-fourteenth century Giovanni Boccaccio (1313–75) wrote the *Decameron*, a collection of one-hundred stories shared among ten acquaintances who fled Florence during a plague. The parallels to the COVID-19 pandemic, and especially the isolation and social distancing phenomena experienced worldwide, resonated with Music Division staff.

Drawing on Boccaccio's example, the Library asked ten pairs of composers and performers to write and perform brief solo works; these premiered online over the course of ten weekdays in June 2020. The artists self-produced videos using whatever means were available to them, showing at once the intensity of forced separation and the unity of spirit in the arts community's response to it. Each of the collaborations was heartfelt and impressive, moving from composition to recorded performance within a matter of weeks. To open the collection, pianist Jeremy Jordan performed Damien Sneed's *Sequestered Thoughts*, recorded and self-produced on two phones. In Erin Lesser's performance of Erin Rogers' work *Hello World*, only a microphone and the color-manipulated skin of the flutist, which is a neon chartreuse against a blue background, is visible. The effect is striking, as the artist strives to be heard and seen. The set closed with a composition by Allison Loggins-Hull, who wrote for Nathalie Joachim—her partner in the duo Flutronix—a work called *Have and Hold* for flute, voice, and electronics. Filmed in Joachim's apartment, the closeup of the musician smiling, hand to her heart, offered a sense of hope at a time when it was especially needed. The isolation that took over during the pandemic clarified the essential role of the audience in the Library's music-making enterprises—the reception of a trusting public has allowed the series to flourish with its vibrant programming and unique ability to contextualize music, regardless of the circumstances.

Orpheus Chamber Orchestra performed the world premiere of Danny Elfman's Suite for chamber orchestra, co-commissioned by the Library of Congress, Los Angeles Chamber Orchestra, and National Symphony Orchestra of Ireland. The concert took place at St. Mark's Episcopal Church, Washington, DC, May 4, 2023, while the Coolidge Auditorium was undergoing repairs following a flood on December 24, 2022.

Act II

New Horizons

Scene 1: Reaching Across America

Bass-baritone Thomas Hampson performs in the Coolidge Auditorium for Poets & Patriotism: The 200th Birthday of the Star-Spangled Banner concert on July 3, 2014.

From the inception of the concert series, the Music Division has worked to maximize its reach. The series rapidly developed a global reputation through its innovative efforts to make concerts available through emerging technologies—such as terrestrial radio in the 1920s, the internet beginning in the 1990s, and satellite radio in the early 2000s—and quickly became a highly coveted booking for the top touring classical musicians. The division chief and concert staff also engaged international partner nations for cultural diplomacy collaborations. The concerts remain attractive social events among music lovers and Washington's social elite, including frequent attendance by members of Congress, the foreign diplomatic corps, and senior federal officials. This level of visibility helped attract embassies and cultural organizations to collaborate with the Music Division and to promote artistic exchange between the United States and other nations—making the concert series an integral component of the Library's work in cultural diplomacy.

In addition to the Music Division's series, the concert staff also lends expertise to major Library initiatives, producing concerts, festivals, and special events that engage communities with the Library's collections, exhibitions, institutional partnerships, and services. While Coolidge was clear that the Coolidge Auditorium was "planned for and dedicated to the performance of chamber music," she also envisioned the Music Division's contribution to the broader agency by specifying that the hall could "...also be available... for any other suitable purpose, secondary to the needs of the Music Division."

The Coolidge Auditorium was designed with radio broadcast in mind (at its benefactor's insistence), and the Library broadcasted concerts into the living rooms and cars of America for most of the twentieth century and into the twenty-first century. Between the 1920s and 1990s, the Concerts from the Library of Congress radio series provided a direct connection between the American people and their national library, reaching up to 150 major markets with live performances on a weekly basis. Even as the internet age began to subsume radio, the Music Division continued to create broadcast packages for national distribution, produced in partnership with WETA and featuring Bill McGlaughlin as host, in addition to partnering with new models of radio distribution including SiriusXM satellite radio and WNYC/WQXR's online station Q2 music (which evolved into the New Sounds online station in 2018). This vision for expanding the reach of cultural activities presented at the Library continues to have an impact in the twenty-first century with the growth of the Library's digital presence, social media, and television and streaming projects, such as the annual concert celebrating the recipient of the Library of Congress Gershwin Prize for Popular Song.

"To NBC's executives I wish to express my gratitude for the splendid victory for chamber music over those doubts and misgivings which at first confronted my insistent and obstinate idea of broadcasting it to the largest possible audience, by the best possible performance of the best possible music; and doing this freely and frequently until we cannot live without it, thus serving Art through Mankind by serving Mankind through Art."

—Elizabeth Sprague Coolidge

Promotional flier sent to radio stations for a 1989-1990 series of archival concert brodcasts.

As technology improved to allow video streaming, the Music Division made visual content available on demand worldwide. This was especially important during the early parts of the COVID-19 pandemic; the concert series adapted swiftly to present full seasons virtually. Multidisciplinary projects, like a virtual performance of George Gershwin's *Rhapsody in Blue* (1924) featuring solo piano and tap dance, provided unique content for online audiences.

Concert Recordings

An essential function of the concert series is creating content for the Library's collections, and, when possible, making the recordings available to global audiences through online radio platforms, commercial recording releases, and on the Library's digital media platforms. Audio and video recordings of concerts form an important archival body for researchers and for the preservation of America's cultural heritage. These recordings include interviews with composers and performers, rare recordings of leading ensembles and soloists, and evidence of performance practice in Western classical music and jazz. The recordings also offer opportunities to hear the Library's historic instruments—principally the Stradivari string instruments—and the glorious auditorium acoustics in the hands of world-renowned artists.

Beginning in 2007, analog and digital recordings of concerts and

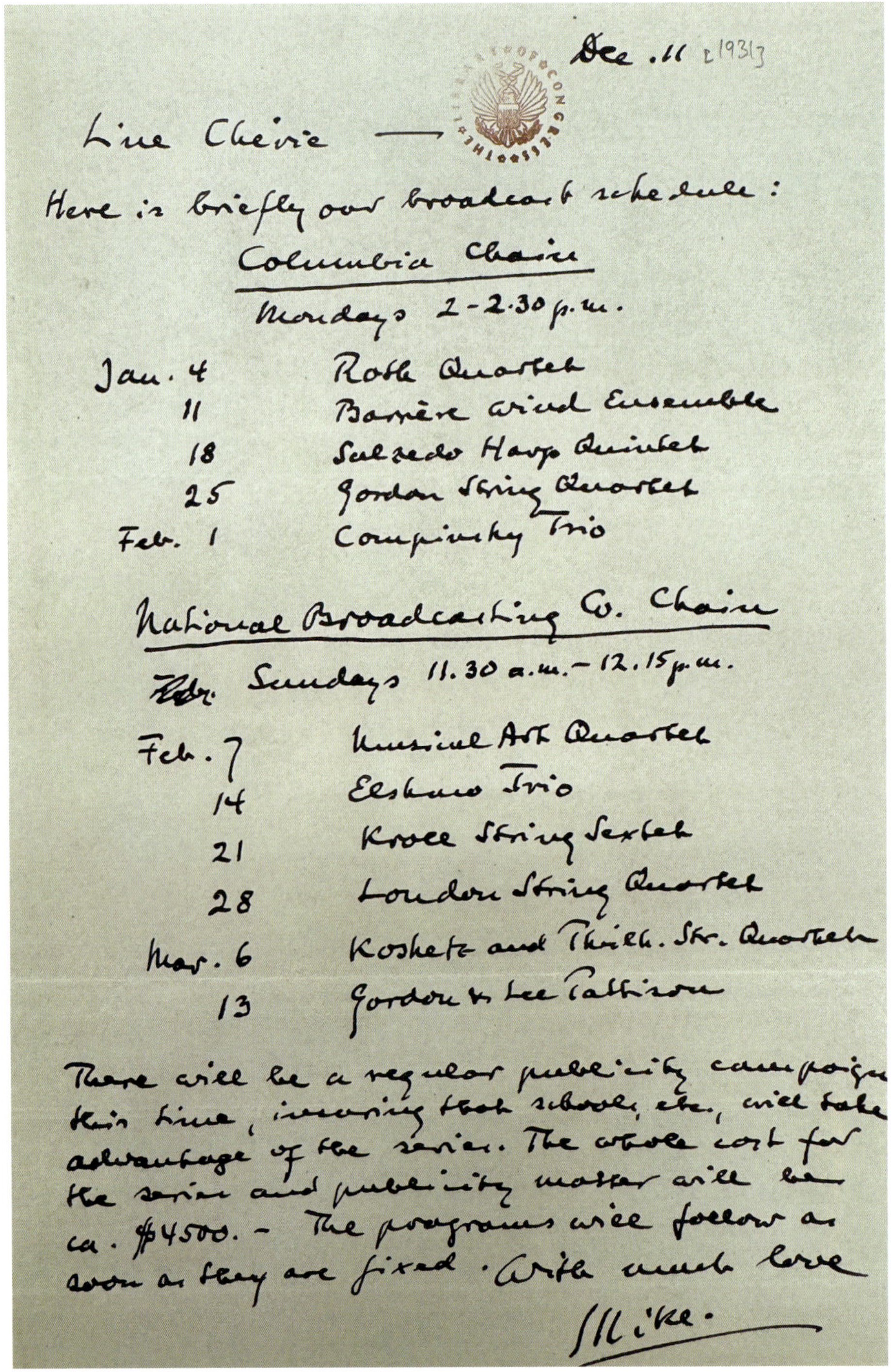

Dec. 11 [1931]

Liebe Chérie —

Here is briefly our broadcast schedule:

Columbia Chain

Mondays 2-2.30 p.m.

Jan. 4 Roth Quartet
11 Barrère Wind Ensemble
18 Salzedo Harp Quintet
25 Gordon String Quartet
Feb. 1 Compinsky Trio

National Broadcasting Co. Chain

Sundays 11.30 a.m.–12.15 p.m.

Feb. 7 Musical Art Quartet
14 Elshuco Trio
21 Kroll String Sextet
28 London String Quartet
Mar. 6 Koshetz and Thrill. Str. Quartet
13 Gordon & Lee Pattison

There will be a regular publicity campaign this time, insuring that schools, etc., will take advantage of the series. The whole cost for the series and publicity matter will be ca. $4500.– The programs will follow as soon as they are fixed. With much love

Mike.

Left: Note from "Mike" (Carl Engel) to Elizabeth Sprague Coolidge ("Line"), December 11, 1931, describing the Library's forthcoming concert broadcast schedule on "Columbia" (CBS) and "National Broadcasting Company" (NBC).

Above: Pianist Conrad Tao and tap dancer Caleb Teicher present a virtual performance of George Gershwin's *Rhapsody in Blue* during the COVID-19 pandemic when in-person concerts were on hiatus for safety reasons. Released on April 23, 2021.

programs are preserved at the Library's National Audio-Visual Conservation Center in Culpeper, Virginia. The Music Division was the original custodian of these recordings and the Library's commercial and archival audio holdings, which were transferred to the Motion Picture and Recorded Sound Division (now part of the National Audiovisual Conservation Center) in 1978. Selected audio and video recordings of concerts are distributed via the Library's website and other third-party platforms to promote engagement with the collections.

Commercial recordings of numerous live performances and special productions have also been a staple in the output of the concert series, always in collaboration with a record label. The Bridge Records series Great Performances from the Library of Congress comprises more than two dozen albums with performances ranging from the Budapest String Quartet and soprano Dorthy Maynor to Leopold Stokowski conducting

Havana-born jazz vocalist and composer Daymé Arocena demonstrates Afro-Cuban influences in music in an educational video released on October 15, 2021. A highlight of the concert series' pandemic-era presentations was an extensive series of educational videos. These productions helped sustain artists during the height of COVID-19 public health restrictions and provided engaging content for listeners. The videos, available at loc.gov/concerts, feature acts such as Tank and the Bangas, Argentinean pianist and composer Pablo Ziegler on traditional and nuevo tango, and Ranky Tanky on Contemporary Gullah Songs.

the Symphony of the Air and Aaron Copland's eighty-first birthday concert with Jan DeGaetani and Leo Smit. The series launched in 1996 with a recording of the Budapest String Quartet and Cleveland Orchestra conductor George Szell in a rare performance at the piano performing the Brahms Piano Quintet, op. 34, and Schubert's "Trout Quintet," op. 114, D. 667.

Military Bands

The metropolitan Washington, DC, area is home to five of the US armed forces' premier military bands. Throughout the history of the concert series, these ensembles have performed evening-length programs in the Coolidge Auditorium and supported special ceremonial events in the Jefferson Building. These bands are filled with outstanding, versatile musicians who are highly skilled at transitioning between artistic, ceremonial, and entertainment roles. Notable appearances in the early 2000s include "The President's Own" United States Marine Band's performance of "Music in the Lincoln White House" for the Civil War Sesquicentennial on February 9, 2013; the US Army Blues' performance as part of composer/conductor John Adams's week-long residency on May 25, 2013; the US Navy Band's performance of works by Giovanni Gabrieli and Carlo Gesualdo for the October 20, 2013, Founder's Day Concert; and the US Air Force Band's appearance with Simone Dinnerstein for the one-hundredth anniversary of George Gershwin's

Top: CD cover of *Leontyne Price & Samuel Barber: Historic Performances 1938 & 1953*, vol. 19 of the Great Performances from the Library of Congress series, Bridge Records 9156, 2004). Leontyne Price and Samuel Barber performed the world premiere of Barber's *Hermit Songs* (October 30, 1953), an Elizabeth Sprague Coolidge Foundation Commission, in the Coolidge Auditorium.

Middle: CD cover of *Aaron Copland 81st Birthday Concert at the Library of Congress: Jan DeGaetani, Leo Smit*, recorded November 14, 1981, Bridge Records 9046 (1993).

Bottom: "The President's Own" United States Marine Band under the direction of Col. Michael J. Colburn perform "Music in the Lincoln White House" with guest presenter Professor Allen Guelzo of Gettysburg College, Coolidge Auditorium, February 9, 2013.

The United States Army Old Guard Fife and Drum Corps performed at the Live! At the Library: A Martha Washington and Queen Charlotte Regency Ball, which marked the public opening of the Two Georges: Parallel Lives in An Age of Revolution exhibition, March 27, 2025.

"The President's Own" United States Marine Band performs in the Great Hall in celebration of a major donation of Sousa manuscripts by the Sousa family, Thomas Jefferson Building, November 16, 1953.

Rhapsody in Blue on February 12, 2024. The Library has also hosted performances by the US Army Herald Trumpets, the US Army Strings, the Air Force Strings, chamber ensembles from "the President's Own," and the US Coast Guard Band from New London, Connecticut. The American military band tradition, which honors the central role of music in American civic life, holds a special connection to the Music Division, which is the home of the John Philip Sousa Papers and the piccolo used to premiere *The Stars and Stripes Forever*, as well as the papers of Francis Maria Scala, leader of the Marine Band during the Civil War.

Cultural Diplomacy

A hallmark of life in the nation's capital is the presence and visibility of diplomatic delegations from around the world. The active presence of embassies fosters endless possibilities for bilateral cultural collaborations, and the concert series has benefitted from numerous partnerships with embassies and delegations. Engagement between the Library and diplomats was established as a precedent by Coolidge, who ensured that ambassadors and senior diplomats were invited to the concerts from the beginning. These diplomatic relationships served to sustain relationships with cultural institutions in other countries. Coolidge sponsored European tours for some of the ensembles she supported, such as the Coolidge Quartet. Her connections in Europe also provided important recommendations about composers who were deserving of her consideration for new commissions.

European delegations, ranging from the European Union to the Embassy of France and the government of Catalunya (Spain), have a major presence in the history of the concert series. Embassies and their affiliated cultural organizations, such as the Italian Cultural Institute of Washington, often provide financial or promotional support for concerts showcasing artists or composers from their nations. The diplomatic delegations may be involved as co-presenters of concerts or more casually by helping to bring out their local expatriate community to concerts of interest at the Library.

The Embassy of Italy and the Italian Cultural Institute are longstanding partners of the concert series. This special association exists because of the Music Division's collection strengths in rare editions and manuscripts of Italian operas, as well as its significant archival

The Quartetto di Cremona with the Library of Congress Stradivari instrument collection. The quartet perfomed on May 11, 2018, co-presented by the Library, the Embassy of Italy, and the Italian Cultural Institute. The ensemble regularly performs on four Stradivari instruments, known as the "Paganini Quartet," making their appearance with the Library's instruments a significant reunion of Stradivari instruments.

holdings of twentieth-century Italian modernist composers, such as Mario Castelnuovo-Tedesco and Luigi Dallapiccola. The Library's role as a preeminent steward of Cremonese stringed instruments, such as those made by Stradivari, Guarneri, and Amati, likewise makes the Italian government a natural collaborator, since these instruments represent one of Italy's greatest contributions to Western civilization.

There is also a history of cooperation with the Embassy of Japan, which co-presented a performance of the Shigeyama Kyogen Troupe on March 21, 2017, and cultural organizations promoting Russian and American engagement. Russian ambassador to the United States Sergey H. Kislyak presided over the Library's "Celebration of Russia" in November 2012, a co-presentation with American University's Initiative for Russian Culture and the Mariinsky Foundation of America. The event featured performances by pianist Denis Matsuev, Valery Gergiev, and the Mariinsky Orchestra.

Top: Depiction of a Kyōgen play from the Library's collection of Japanese Fine Prints, nineteenth century.

Bottom: Shigeyama Kyogen Troupe performs in the Coolidge Auditorium, March 17, 2017. This event illustrates how Concerts from the Library of Congress provides a platform for showcasing the Library's collections and reinterpretations of global music, dance, and theater traditions.

Opposite page, top: From left to right: Marjorie Billington, Vice Admiral Sir Tim Laurence, Her Royal Highness Princess Anne, Princess Royal, and Dr. James H. Billington at the opening ceremony for the Library of Congress exhibition Magna Carta: Muse and Mentor, in the Great Hall, Thomas Jefferson Building, November 6, 2014. Concert series staff curated the musical performances and music production elements for the exhibition's opening ceremony as well as the gala program in the Coolidge Auditorium.

Opposite page, bottom left: Temple Church Choir, Roger Sayer, director, performs at the opening gala for the Magna Carta exhibition opening, Coolidge Auditorium, November 6, 2014.

Opposite page, bottom right: American mezzo-soprano Denyce Graves Montgomery and pianist Laura Ward perform in the Coolidge Auditorium during the Magna Carta exhibition gala program, representing musical exchange between the United States and United Kingdom.

This page: Cellist Ulrich Heinen of Birmingham Contemporary Music Group in rehearsal with composer/conductor Oliver Knussen, April 4, 2014, Coolidge Auditorium. Heinen holds the Library's Stradivari "Castelbarco" cello from 1699.

Rule, Brittania!

The Library maintains a special multifaceted relationship with the government of the United Kingdom, the Royal Family, British Council USA, and contemporary British composers and performers that spans the entire history of Concerts from the Library of Congress. The strong diplomatic and cultural friendship has benefited the American people and users of the Library's collections through exhibitions, collection acquisitions, and cultural events. Members of the British diplomatic corps have attended concerts in the Coolidge Auditorium since 1925 and have collaborated through sponsorships and promotional support to showcase the music, composers, and performers who contribute to the United Kingdom's rich musical history. Music Division staff frequently help develop artistic programming for ceremonial and diplomatic events at the Library, providing visibility for the performing arts collections and concert series in historical moments for the institution.

In November 2014, the Temple Church Choir led by Roger Sayer, opera star Denyce Graves-Montgomery, and the US Army Herald Trumpets performed in the Great Hall to commemorate the eight-hundredth anniversary of the first issue of the Magna Carta and the arrival of the Lincoln (UK) Cathedral King John Magna Carta, which the Library held for

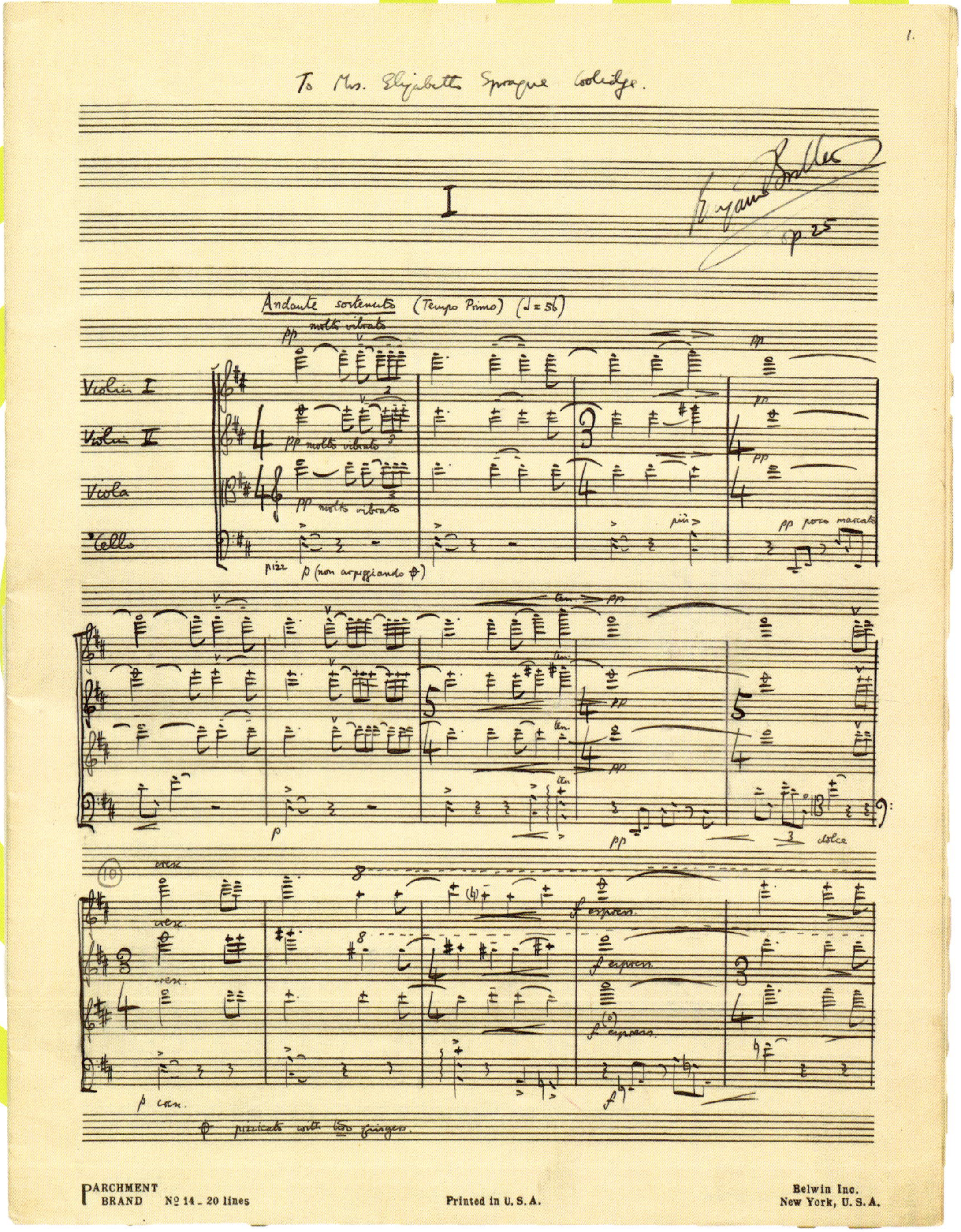

Left: Manuscript of Benjamin Britten's String Quartet no. 1 in D major, op. 25 (1941), commissioned by the Elizabeth Sprague Coolidge Foundation. The East Coast premiere of the quartet was given in the Coolidge Auditorium by the Coolidge Quartet with Britten in attendance.

Opposite page: Letter from Benjamin Britten introducing himself to Coolidge, September, 1939. Britten shared a letter of introduction with Coolidge from his composition teacher Frank Bridge, who had also been a beneficiary of Coolidge's patronage. Peter Pears, CBE, who was Britten's partner, performed a concert in memory of Britten at the Library on March 25, 1980.

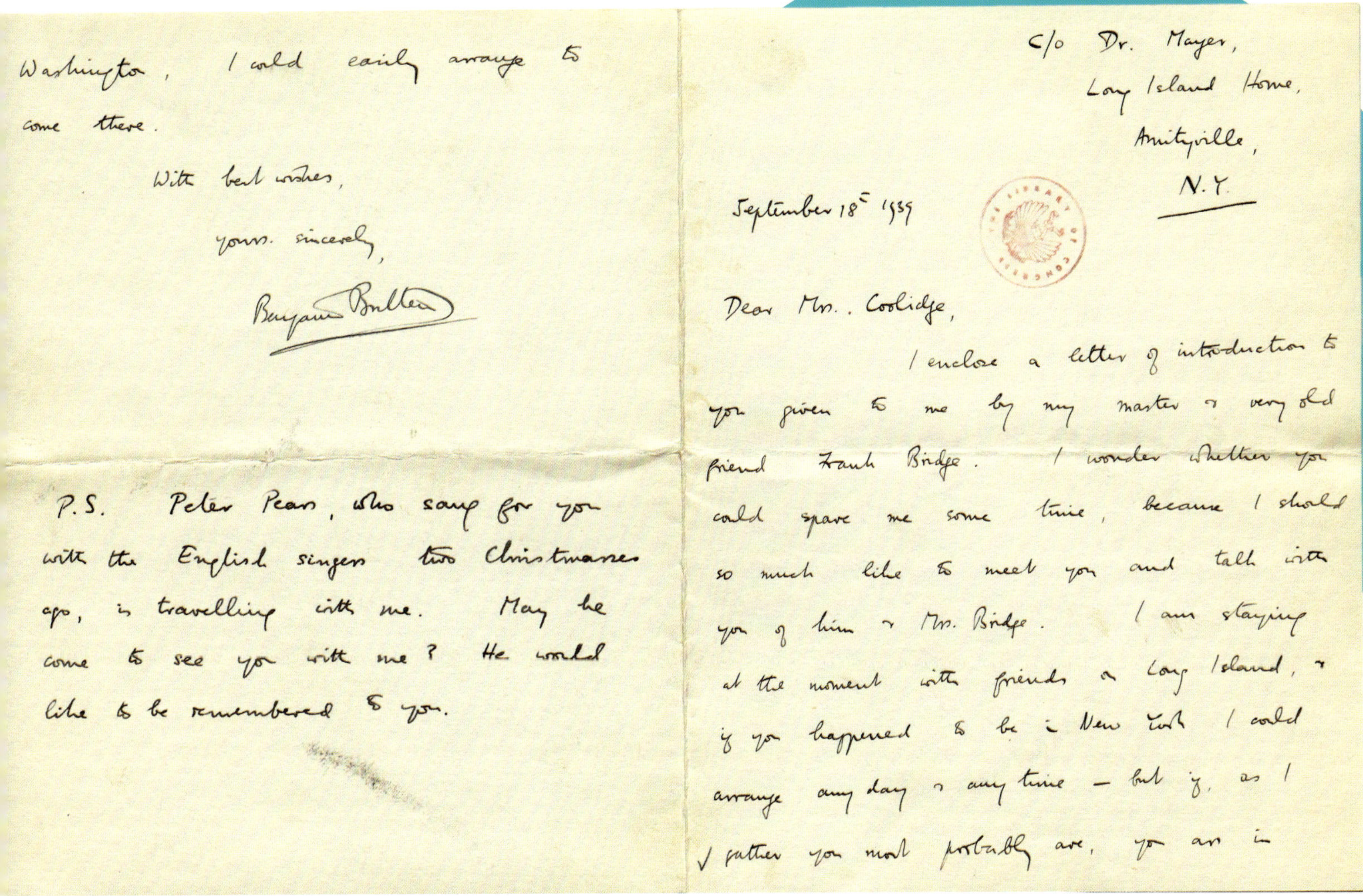

Washington, I could easily arrange to come there.

With best wishes,

yours sincerely,

Benjamin Britten

P.S. Peter Pears, who sang for you with the English singers two Christmasses ago, is travelling with me. May he come to see you with me? He would like to be remembered to you.

c/o Dr. Mayer,
Long Island Home,
Amityville,
N.Y.

September 18th 1939

Dear Mrs. Coolidge,

I enclose a letter of introduction to you given to me by my master & very old friend Frank Bridge. I wonder whether you could spare me some time, because I should so much like to meet you and talk with you of him & Mrs. Bridge. I am staying at the moment with friends on Long Island, & if you happened to be in New York I could arrange any day & any time – but if, as I gather you most probably are, you are in

safekeeping on behalf of the British during World War II and displayed in the *Magna Carta: Muse and Mentor* exhibition. The occasion was marked with an official visit from Her Royal Highness The Princess Anne, Princess Royal and Vice Admiral Sir Tim Laurence.

The Oliver Knussen Residency, held Aprill 7–12, 2014, was a collaboration with British Council USA, featuring appearances by Birmingham Contemporary Music Group, composer/conductor Oliver Knussen, and composer/pianist Huw Watkins. Concerts featured works by Knussen, Benjamin Britten, and Frank Bridge (both Coolidge commission recipients), the regional premiere of Elliott Carter's final work, *Epigrams* for piano trio and the world premiere of Marc Neikrug's *Tiger's Nest*, commissioned by the Dina Koston and Roger Shapiro Fund for New Music.

Exploring Latin American Music

Latin American music and dance have been featured throughout the history of the concert series, providing an important avenue for the Library of Congress to engage in cultural diplomacy with partner countries who are also members of the Organization of American States and represent strategic interests for the US government, such as the important bilateral relationship with Mexico. From commissioning influential Mexican composer Carlos Chávez's *Dark Meadow* (1943–44) ballet score for the Martha Graham Dance Company to Peruvian American composer Gabriela Lena Frank's oratorio *My Angel, His Name is Freedom* (2015), the Library has contributed to the expansion of classical repertoire influenced by the many cultures and identities represented in the Latin American cultural diaspora.

Between 1958 and 1983, the Music Division co-presented events in the Coolidge Auditorium for the semiannual Inter-American Music Festival organized by the Inter-American Music Council under the auspices of the Pan American Union. First Lady Jacqueline Kennedy served as the inaugural chair for the 1961 festival, a role that was later passed to President Lyndon Johnson and First Lady "Lady Bird" Johnson. The festivals featured performances by musicians from Latin nations and the United States in repertoire of Latin composers such as Roque Cordero (Panama) and Enrique Solares (Guatemala), and Americans, including Aaron Copland. The stated aim of the 1961 festival was "to promote closer relations and understanding among the American republics by recognizing and stimulating the development of ... Music of the Americas."

> *"The underlying message—one that has persisted since well before the first such event in 1958—was that music has no north or south, east or west. It knows no geographical bounds, for its language is universal."*
>
> —Charles McCardell, *The Washington Post*, April 30, 1983

Top: Program from the second Inter-American Music Festival (1961), Washington, DC.

Opposite page and this page, bottom: Maru Montero Dance Company (opposite page) and Cuarteto Latinoamericano (this page, bottom) performing traditional and contemporary Mexican works during "A Celebration of Mexico" on December 12, 2013, a co-presentation between the Library and the Embassy of Mexico, curated by Senior Advisor to the Librarian of Congress Marie Arana. The multidisciplinary convening also featured talks by author Sandra Cisneros and journalist María Hinojosa.

Top: Stevie Wonder performs during the Gershwin Prize for Popular Song concert that honored him in the Coolidge Auditorium, February 23, 2009. Wonder received a commission from the McKim Fund in the Library of Congress for his work *Sketches of a Life*, which premiered in the Coolidge Auditorium on February 23, 2009.

Left: Gershwin Prize honoree Joni Mitchell plays on George Gershwin's Steinway piano in the Thomas Jefferson Building, May 2, 2023.

Opposite page, top: 2019 Gershwin Prize honoree Gloria Estefan performs with her daughter, Emily, during the Gershwin Prize concert honoring Gloria and Emilio Estefan at DAR Constitution Hall, March 13, 2019.

Opposite page, background: Jacob Lusk of Gabriels performs during the Gershwin Prize for Popular Song tribute concert honoring Elton John and Bernie Taupin, March 20, 2024.

A Legacy of American Song: The Library of Congress Gershwin Prize for Popular Song

Inaugurated in 2007, the Library of Congress Gershwin Prize for Popular Song is the nation's highest award for influence, impact, and achievement in the field of popular song. It honors the artists whose creative works, both printed and recorded, are collected, preserved, made accessible, and valued by the nation's library. It acknowledges the preeminent place of popular song in modern society and its vital role in expressing and deepening the personal and shared values of our time.

Honorees represent genres from Latin pop to rock and roll. After spending several days at the Library learning about the collections and its efforts to preserve American musical heritage, honorees are feted with an all-star tribute concert featuring performances of their music by international superstars. The Gershwin Prize concert broadcasts reach audiences nationwide and throughout Canada. The show was presented in conjunction with the White House between 2009 and 2013, and the award is presented jointly by the Librarian of Congress and congressional leadership.

Gershwin Prize Honorees Through 2024

2007
Paul Simon

2009
Stevie Wonder

2010
Paul McCartney

2012
Burt Bacharach & Hal David

2013
Carole King

2014
Billy Joel

2015
Willie Nelson

2016
Smokey Robinson

2017
Tony Bennett

2019
Gloria & Emilio Estefan

2020
Garth Brooks

2022
Lionel Richie

2023
Joni Mitchell

2024
Elton John & Bernie Taupin

Bibliodiscotheque

In 2015, Gloria Gaynor's iconic song "I Will Survive" (written by Dino Fekaris) was inducted into the Library of Congress National Recording Registry, which was established in 2002 to preserve American history through important recordings of songs, speeches, podcasts, or recorded sounds that reflect the nation's cultural heritage. The news created so much viral buzz on social media that Deputy Librarian of Congress Robert R. Newlen invited the Music Division to develop a project to showcase the legendary disco number. What resulted was Library of Congress Bibliodiscotheque, a transformative moment in the history of the Library's efforts to connect with the American people. Disco music is renowned for bringing together people from all backgrounds to feel the spirit of the beat. The month-long celebration featured scholarly programs about the African roots of American popular dance since the 1970s; a conversation about fashion with Tim Gunn; screenings of popular films known for their representation of dance; a symposium on the influence of the disco era featuring *Good Morning America* co-anchor Robin Roberts' interview with Gaynor; and talks by mirror ball maker Yolanda Baker and photographer Bill Bernstein, who covered the disco scene for the *Village Voice* in the 1970s and early 1980s. The series showcased a spectacular closing concert with a capacity-crowd featuring Gaynor in the Great Hall and was presented in collaboration with BrightestYoungThings, the Recording Academy, Capital Pride, and the DC Library Association.

Above: Gloria Gaynor performs in the Great Hall of the Thomas Jefferson Building as part of the Bibliodiscotheque series, May 6, 2017. **Opposite page, top:** Fashion expert Tim Gunn (on right) discusses disco fashion with Deputy Librarian of Congress Robert R. Newlen, who shows off a platform shoe from the disco era, May 2, 2017. **Opposite page, middle:** Librarian of Congress Carla Hayden, in her disco wig, dances in the Great Hall during "Gloria Gaynor: Disco Dance Party," May 6, 2017. **Opposite page, bottom:** Former Second Lady of the United States Mary Elizabeth "Tipper" Gore during "silent disco," presented by Sandro Kereselidze (founder and creative director, Artechouse) in the Main Reading Room, Thomas Jefferson Building, during the "Gloria Gaynor: Disco Dance Party," May 6, 2017.

Popular Song – ASCAP and CMA

American popular song has always been featured in the Library's concert series. Folk music and spirituals in the 1920s were later followed by country, R&B, and pop on the Coolidge stage, connecting contemporary genres to the Western music traditions represented in the Music Division's collections. Concert collaborations with the Country Music Association (CMA) and the American Society of Composers, Authors, and Publishers (ASCAP) began in the 2010s, providing support for the Library to showcase the important work of American songwriters across musical genres.

The ASCAP We Write the Songs concerts were developed after the ASCAP Foundation donated the organization's archives of creators' works in 2019, representing more than 275,000 creators who were ASCAP members, including Victor Herbert, Leonard Bernstein, George and Ira Gershwin, and Vernon Duke. For each concert, ASCAP invites a cross-section of its distinguished member singer-songwriters to perform at the Library. Established and emerging songwriters perform their own songs, including Reba McIntire, Paul Williams, Randy Newman, and Stevie Wonder. At each concert, at least one of the performing singer-songwriters donates additional materials to the ASCAP Collection at the Library. The longstanding relationship with ASCAP is particularly relevant to the growth of the Music Division's special collections. The papers of Victor Herbert—one of ASCAP's

US Senator Tim Kaine (Virginia) gave a cameo performance on harmonica during the May 16, 2018, ASCAP We Write the Songs Concert, featuring Jason Mraz. The concerts feature performances by leading songwriters across popular song genres. Each songwriter is introduced by one of their hometown members of Congress. In hosting the ASCAP We Write the Songs concerts, the Library provides a distinctive opportunity for artists and elected officials to connect through live performance.

founders—were acquired from the 1920s through the late 1950s, followed by the papers of numerous ASCAP composers and songwriters, including those of Burt Bacharach in 2024.

The Concerts from the Library of Congress series collaborated with the CMA between 2010 and 2016 to present a CMA's Songwriters' Series event in the Coolidge Auditorium. These intimate concerts brought prominent and emerging country music singer-songwriters to the Library to perform in a songwriters circle format, with several artists on stage trading off performing some of their popular or lesser-known works. The CMA collaboration was the first time country music was regularly featured on the series. Collaborations with organizations like ASCAP and CMA provide opportunities for the concert series to showcase genres beyond those supported by available gift and trust funds, which have historically focused on supporting classical music. The concerts have also served to expand the audience for the concert series as contemporary popular music was incorporated through these specific partnerships.

Top: Country music stars Bob DiPiero, Clint Black, and Patty Loveless perform as part of the Country Music Association Songwriters Series, Coolidge Auditorium, November 16, 2011. The CMA arranges for major country music artists and songwriters to perform at the Library for audiences that include elected officials, music industry leaders, and the public. The Library provides a platform for celebrating the cultural contributions of these artists and preserves their performances for the collections. **Bottom:** Jimmy Jam (left) and Terry Lewis perform during the 2023 ASCAP We Write the Songs concert at the Library, September 19, 2023.

Scene 2: Creating Community

As America's library, the Library of Congress serves as a gathering place for anyone to come together to experience the stories of our past, present, and future. The sense of community this inspires is a hallmark of the Concerts from the Library of Congress experience for concertgoers, staff, supporters, and volunteers alike. While staff manage concert production, the box office, and front of house operations, volunteer ushers contribute hundreds of hours each season to help provide a welcoming environment for concertgoers. Volunteer ushers come from all walks of life, including students receiving service credit, retired Library of Congress staff, and dedicated music lovers. Several volunteer ushers have been a regular presence in the Coolidge Auditorium for twenty years or more and offer new and returning concertgoers a sense of belonging.

The concerts are fully funded through the gifts of generous donors. As radio broadcasts and digital content take the Library's collections to the furthest corners of the United States, the live concerts bring people together for the magical act of being in community while having a deeply personal listening experience. The variety of genres and artists presented ensures that the series attracts a diverse audience; on a typical night, an international visitor might be seated next to a featured composer, who is seated next to a member of Congress and a music student. The act of listening to music in the Coolidge Auditorium's pristine acoustic, accompanied by representative treasures from the collection, makes for a unique experience. What further distinguishes the concert series from others is that the Library offers this musical alchemy on a weekly basis from October to June.

> ***"What makes the concerts especially meaningful are the lobby displays of memorabilia from the Music Division's collections, whether it be a composer's handwritten score, letters, or other objects related to each event. The lives and works of the music creators [and] performers become more immediate and compelling, adding to one's enjoyment of the sounds performed live. Indeed, I can't imagine the concerts without these magical objects."***
>
> —Volunteer usher Lorna Grenadier

Concertgoers view a display of manuscripts and programs in the Coolidge Auditorium lobby prior to attending the Stradivari Anniversary Concert featuring the Pacifica Quartet on December 18, 2024.

The Friends of Music in the Library of Congress

By Loras John Schissel,
Senior Music Specialist, Music Division

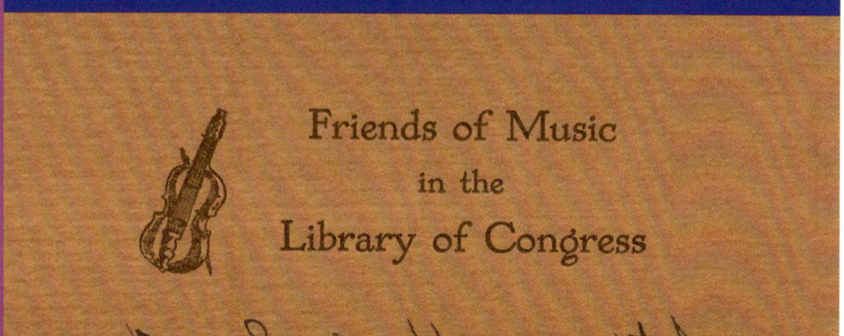

During the early years of the concert series, Music Division Chief Carl Engel and Elizabeth Sprague Coolidge regularly corresponded about the finances of the concerts, as the joint artistic vision of the two impresarios sometimes required funds beyond the income generated from Coolidge's trust fund. Out of that need, and the buzz generated by the concerts in society and artistic circles, the Friends of Music was organized on December 11, 1928, with the following goals:

1. *To provide a link among serious music lovers all over the country by associating them, through our National Library, in musical activities devoted wholly to artistic and educational ends.*

2. *To provide funds for the purchase and gift of additions to the music collections in the Library of Congress, such as historical rarities, significant publications, and manuscripts, old and contemporaneous.*

3. *To provide [access to], for members of the association, concerts to which the richness of the national music collection will contribute unusual musical significance.*

The association grew out of the Chamber Music Society of Washington, which was not formally affiliated with the Library of Congress, but which was the brainchild of Engel. Beginning in 1924, through subscription, members enjoyed several yearly chamber music concerts performed in members' homes. Engel and a small committee would select an interesting program featuring unique materials from the collections of the Library and performed by artists of international renown. To keep the focus on the music itself, Engel went so far as to have the performers play from behind a screen, and the printed program always carried the admonishment: "The performing artists will be presented to the audience at the *end* of the concert." Engel's encyclopedic knowledge of chamber music informed his highly interesting programs of unusual breadth and variety.

Above: Presentation of music manuscripts acquired by the Friends of Music in the Library of Congress to Library officials on May 7, 1930, Northwest Courtyard, adjacent to the Coolidge Auditorium, Thomas Jefferson Building. From left to right: Dr. Carl Engel, Chief of the Music Division; Herbert Putnam, Librarian of Congress; Speaker of the House Nicholas Longworth, President, Friends of Music in the Library of Congress; Mary Carlisle Howe, composer, pianist, philanthropist and vice president, Friends of Music; Grace Dunham Guest, assistant curator of the Freer Gallery at the Smithsonian Institution and secretary, Friends of Music; Henry Barrett Learned, historian, educator, and treasurer, Friends of Music; and Frank J. Frost, banking and oil executive and associate treasurer, Friends of Music.

Opposite page: Serge Koussevitzky's non-resident membership card for the Friends of Music in the Library of Congress, 1931.

The advent of the Library's concert series funded by the Coolidge Foundation led to the demise of the society in 1928, as Engel provided a more formal platform for enjoying chamber music via the Library. The Friends of Music was modeled after the Gesellschaft der Musikfreunde in Vienna (founded in 1814). The first president of the Friends was none other than Speaker of the House Nicholas Longworth of the US House of Representatives, who was himself a violinist and devoted music lover. Its members served as a dedicated group of boosters who championed the series, provided supplemental financial support, and regularly attended the concerts. For many years, there was a certain prestige associated with joining the cause of free chamber music for the public, with supporters joining from as far away as Massachusetts (including Boston Symphony Orchestra conductor Serge Koussevitzky). Alice Roosevelt Longworth, the eldest daughter of President Theodore Roosevelt and Longworth's wife, was also an influential early member of the Friends.

Of the many gifts by the Friends over the years, of particular note was the purchase of the complete full score of the opera *Wozzeck*, in the hand of its composer, Alban Berg. The Friends of Music also awarded annual gifts to the concert series between 1929 and 1941. Due to the exigencies of World War II, the Friends suspended its activities. In 1942, the remaining monies in its treasury were transferred to the Library of Congress Trust Fund Board.

The Friends of Music continues to exist today as a collective of dedicated concertgoers and supporters whose multi-year commitment to the series is essential to its longevity. The original trust fund transferred to the Library remains active in supporting concerts, acquisitions, and commissions. While supporters of the concert series now contribute to a diverse range of funds, their commitment is part of the lineage from the Friends of Music led by Speaker Longworth and others, through annual and planned giving, and service as volunteer ushers for concerts. The Friends of Music program is part of the heritage of the more recent philanthropic community at the Library called the Friends of the Library, which is an initiative of the Librarian's Office that aims to "bring together a community of donors committed to preserving this nation's cultural memory." ■

Top: Nicholas Longworth as a young man playing the violin, from *The Making of Nicholas Longworth: Annals of an American Family* by Clara Longworth de Chambrun.

Bottom: Music Division Chief Susan Vita and longtime supporter Carl Tretter, whose parents first brought him to the Library of Congress for concerts in the 1970s, December 18, 2024.

Luminaries

Elizabeth Sprague Coolidge and Gertrude Clarke Whittall are credited as the founders of philanthropy in the Library of Congress. Their philanthropic leadership, in the years following the ratification of the Nineteenth Amendment to the Constitution, which gave women voting rights, further confirmed that women leaders could make major contributions in the civic and cultural arenas. It is of interest to note that the majority of the concert series' most generous donors since the 1920s and 1930s have been women, such as Leonora Jackson McKim, Carolyn Royall Just, Dina Koston, and Verna Rudnick Fine. There is no discernible evidence for this trend being intentional, though there is extensive scholarship on the role of women, such as Isabella Stewart Gardner, as major collectors in the art world. Each of these supporters followed the role model Coolidge and Whittall provided and shared their commitment to providing the public with free access to performances. Ultimately, the actions of the philanthropists who have established endowments to support the concert series did so because of their sincere trust in the Library's commitment to responsibly steward their gifts for the benefit of the public.

Above: Sarah Coolidge, great-granddaughter of Elizabeth Sprague Coolidge, during a 2024 visit to the Library of Congress. She is standing with two works depicting her great-grandmother, a bronze bust by sculptor Jo Davidson (1934) and a charcoal portrait by John Singer Sargent (1923). **Top right:** Leonora Jackson McKim, standing with violin, September 1891.

Leonora Jackson McKim

Leonora Jackson McKim (1878–1969), the renowned violinist, followed in the footsteps of Coolidge and Whittall after four decades of attending the Library's concerts. Originally from Boston and raised in Chicago, Jackson McKim studied violin in Paris and Berlin, including with Joseph Joachim, the legendary Hungarian violinist, who was a friend of Johannes Brahms and the dedicatee of his violin concerto. She had a distinguished touring career as a soloist and appeared with the Berlin Philharmonic, New York Philharmonic, and Boston Symphony. She famously performed for Queen Victoria at Windsor Castle and won the Mendelssohn State Prize in 1898. The 1714 Stradivari violin is nicknamed the "Leonora Jackson" Stradivarius, as she performed on the instrument during her touring career and owned it from 1906 to 1919.

"Leonora Jackson was the first American violinist whom European opinions recognized to equal any of its great artists and who conquered all the prejudice as to the supposed inferiority of American talent."

—Elena de Sayne, *The Violinist*, November 1923

After marrying her second husband, Dr. W. Duncan McKim, in 1915 and settling in Washington, DC, the couple began to collect art from Europe and the Far East (later donated to the Smithsonian Institution). They also hosted concerts at their home and were dedicated attendees of the Library's concerts, together up until Dr. McKim's death in 1935. In 1969 she established the Leonora Jackson McKim Fund in the Library of Congress, an endowment for the support of commissions and concerts featuring contemporary works for violin and piano by American composers. Jackson McKim's papers are held by the Music Division and include the manuscripts for works commissioned by the fund in the years since her death.

Jackson McKim's endowment at the Library has contributed dozens of substantive works for violin

and piano to the duo repertoire, including several that have been championed by leading touring artists, such as John Adams's *Road Movies* (1995), which has been widely performed by violinists, including Jennifer Koh and Leila Josefowicz. The fund supports composers across genres and has enabled the Library to commission composers ranging from John Cage (*Two4*, 1991) and Esperanza Spalding (*Accompania me me me ment*, 2018) to Ulysses Kay (*Five Portraits*, for violin and piano, 1972) and Ellen Taaffe Zwilich (*Romance*, 1993).

Carolyn Royall Just

Carolyn Royall Just (1906–87) represents the best in the tradition of public service found in the nation's capital, as a career civil service attorney in the US Department of Justice and someone whose planned gift creates opportunities for others to experience live music. Royall Just was born in Shanghai, China, where her parents served as missionaries, and she later made her way to Chicago. Prior to her almost four-decade career in the federal government, Royall Just studied economics, piano, and violin, and even taught herself viola (a common feat among some serious violinists). She was active in the music scene outside of her full-time employment and was a regular attendee of the Library's concerts. The combination of her commitment to public service and love of music led her to bequeath more than $2.3 million to support the performance or broadcasting of classical chamber music concerts in the Coolidge Auditorium. At the time of her passing, this was the largest bequest received to benefit the concert series.

The Carolyn Royall Just Fund in the Library of Congress has provided critical support since the 1990s, including appearances by violist Kim Kashkashian (February 27, 1999), Concerto Köln (March 24, 2000), and the Kronos Quartet's fiftieth anniversary concert (April 18, 2024). The fund has also commissioned several works from the likes of Milton Babbitt (Quartet for piano and strings, 1995) and Jeffrey Mumford (*...amid still and floating depths* for string quartet, 2018, co-commissioned by the Los Angeles Philharmonic Association). Royall Just's legacy helps the Library continue its engagement of large ensembles based in Europe, as well as major soloists and chamber groups.

Opposite page: Tamar Diesendruck, sketches, revisions and signed final version of *Unruly Strands* (2019), commissioned by the McKim Fund and premiered by violinist Midori and pianist Ieva Jokubaviciute. **Above:** Violinist Jennifer Koh and composer Frederic Rzewkski perform the world premiere of Rzewski's *Satires* (2016), a Library of Congress McKim Fund commission, April 30, 2016, Coolidge Auditorium.

Left: Jeffrey Mumford, *...amid still and floating depths*, initialed first page of the computer-generated score for string quartet, 2018. Co-commissioned by the Los Angeles Philharmonic Association and the Dina Koston and Roger Shapiro Fund for New Music in the Library of Congress.

Right: Quartet for piano and strings by Milton Babbitt (1995), holograph manuscript score, page one, commissioned by the Carolyn Royall Just Fund.

Opposite page: Dina Koston, *Duo in Two Parts*, first page. Holograph, commissioned by the McKim Fund in the Library of Congress.

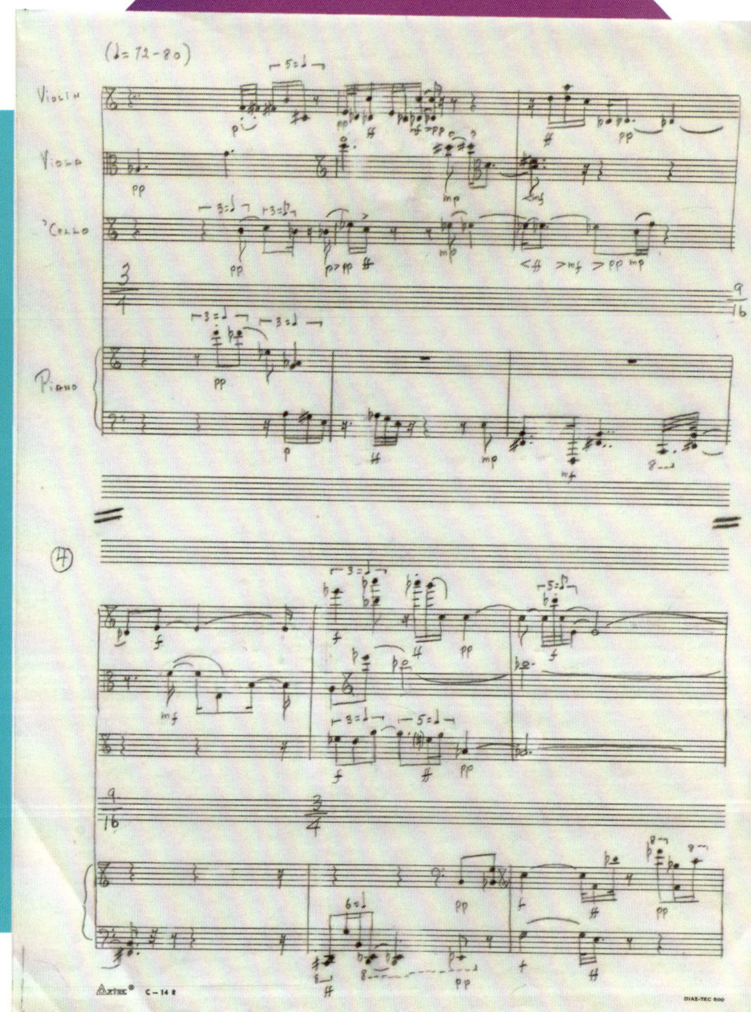

> ***The composer and pianist Dina Koston was one of the driving forces behind new music in Washington for decades."***
>
> – Stephen Brookes, *The Washington Post* (March 8, 2012)

Dina Koston

Composer and pianist Dina Koston (1929–2009) was another influential musical mover and shaker in Washington, DC, whose legacy runs through the Library of Congress' concert series. She and Leon Fleisher created the Theater Chamber Players in 1968, an ensemble of leading musicians in the region that became the Smithsonian Institution's first resident chamber ensemble. The group subsequently became the John F. Kennedy Center for the Performing Arts' resident chamber ensemble in 1978. Koston performed at the Library on several occasions, including for the premiere of her McKim Fund commission *Duo in Two Parts* (1999). Her husband, Roger Shapiro, a psychiatrist, was also a supporter of the arts. Koston established the Dina Koston and Roger Shapiro Fund for New Music in the Library of Congress, through her estate, to provide a legacy of support for contemporary music performances, commissions in the classical tradition, and programs that aligned with the approach of the Theater Chamber Players, combining contemporary music with complementary works from any period. The fund also provided a musical home base for the community of artists and composers who Koston worked with throughout her career.

Iconic American pianist Leon Fleisher marked the inauguration of Koston's fund at the Library with a performance in the Coolidge Auditorium ("Liebeslieder, Ligeti and Koston," March 8, 2012) featuring him, his wife Katherine Jacobson Fleisher, and musicians from the Peabody Institute of the Johns Hopkins University, along with a talk featuring soprano Phyllis Bryn-Julson, a longtime colleague and collaborator of Fleisher's and Koston's.

An Intergenerational Family Affair – Verna Fine and the Fine Family

The Music Division has a long history of cultivating meaningful relationships with numerous composers and their families. This approach has influenced other initiatives at the Library, such as the National Recording Registry and the American Folklife Center's Homegrown Concert Series, which showcases traditional music and dance from around the world. The Library establishes these relationships with artists and creators with an eye toward how their work can be preserved in its collections. An example is the family of composer Irving Fine, which is now on its fourth generation of friendship with the Library. Similar to the Library's connection with the Gershwin family, the collaboration between the Fines and the Music Division has taken many forms over the years.

American composer and educator Irving Fine (1914–62) was a close friend and colleague of Leonard Bernstein and Aaron Copland and a student of Serge Koussevitzky and Nadia Boulanger. Fine arranged the hiring of Bernstein and Copland to the faculty of Brandeis University in Waltham, Massachusetts, where he founded the School of Creative Arts.

Opposite page: Lukas Foss, Verna Fine, Irving Fine, and Harold Shapero at the Tanglewood Music Festival, Lenox, Massachusetts, 1946.

Right: First page of the holograph manuscript of Irving Fine's String Quartet (1952), commissioned by the Koussevitzky Music Foundation in the Library of Congress.

His music is primarily associated with the American neoclassical style, heavily influenced by the work of Igor Stravinsky. Despite an untimely death at age forty-seven, Fine produced a rich and varied collection of works that have become synonymous with his era, including the two sets of *Three Choruses from Alice in Wonderland* (1944 and 1953) and *Partita* for wind quintet (1948).

Fine's awareness of the Library of Congress' concerts grew with his friend Copland's *Appalachian Spring* commission from 1944, the premiere of which he attended. Fine himself received a Koussevitzky Music Foundation commission for his String Quartet (1952). He also corresponded with Coolidge over the years and was awarded a commission for his *Romanza* for wind quintet (1962), which was completed shortly before his death. His widow, Verna Fine (1920–99), maintained a relationship with the Library through her work as an arts administrator, and she donated her late husband's papers between 1964 and 1991. Through her estate, she established the Verna and Irving Fine Endowment in the Library of Congress to support the presentation of concerts, commissions, music history fellowships, and "other research endeavors into the music of Irving Fine and other American composers whose work is also preserved at the Library of Congress."

The Fine Endowment was inaugurated in 2001 with a celebratory concert at the Library featuring conductor Norman Scribner, the Zéphyros Winds, violinist Ida Kavafian, and pianist Ursula Oppens. Bridge Records released a live recording of the concert in 2002 to critical acclaim. In the ensuing decades, Verna and Irving's daughters, and subsequently their grandchildren and great-grandchildren, have championed the concert series and its commissioning of new works, new transcriptions of Fine's works, and new dance works. In passing Fine's music on from generation to generation, the Library exemplifies its ability to influence the repertoire heard on stages around the world. The 2014 Irving Fine Centennial, for example, featured an appearance by the Choir of Clare College, Cambridge, under Graham Ross, and the Martha Graham Company toured Pontus Lidberg's *Woodland* (featuring music by Fine) across Europe, the United States, and Latin America over several seasons following its world premiere at the Library in 2016.

Verna and Irving Fine's daughters Claudia (left), Emily (second from right), and Joanna (right) with artist manager Rosalie Calabrese, Verna Fine's longtime colleague, in the Whittall Pavilion, Thomas Jefferson Building, during a Brandeis University Alumni Association reception held in conjunction with the Library's Irving Fine Centennial Festival in 2014.

A Concertgoing Tradition

By Anne E. McLean, Senior Producer for Concerts and Special Projects, Music Division

Over the past century, audiences and artists alike have found themselves part of a community of music lovers at the Library of Congress. Artists who return to the Coolidge Auditorium throughout their career and the audiences who develop a lifelong practice of attending concerts at the Library often recall how memorable the shared experience is of listening to music in such a hallowed venue. "This is one of the most meaningful things in my life," is a comment often made by longtime patrons; hearing extraordinary music-making in an extraordinary space has created bonds and forged friendships over decades.

Another bond for concertgoers has been the quest for tickets, always in high demand, from the era of letters of inquiry and admittance cards to digital ticketing today. For more than thirty years, beginning in the mid-1960s, that quest involved the camaraderie of a weekly Monday morning trek downtown and a long line that started to form at 6:00 a.m. At the Hayes Concert Bureau, and later at Campbell's Music Store, the genial impresario Patrick Hayes—founder of Washington Performing Arts Society, Inc.—distributed the Library's free tickets, for the very affordable service charge of 25 cents each.

One Library regular joining that line was Dr. Sidney M. Wolfe, cofounder of Public Citizen's Health Research Group, a patron for more than fifty years. "It's been just delightful," he said in a 2015 radio broadcast. "I stood in line—would still stand in line if that were necessary. I love being here! The Coolidge Auditorium is still, to me, the best auditorium in the country in terms of hearing chamber music. It was designed for chamber music in 1925, and it will keep going for a long time. I've been to many other halls, and this one is the best...with the combination of radio broadcasts and enthusiastic audiences, it really helped chamber music take off in this country."

Half a century of concert attendance is not unusual; quite a few patrons have been devoted fans for six decades or longer. One such ardent fan of contemporary music is Geraldine Ostrove, who came to her first Library concert in 1951 at age nine to hear the cellist Gregor Piatigorsky. Ostrove went on to work at the Library of Congress for many years and retired as a senior cataloging policy specialist. Another is Allan Reiter, an avid pianist and chamber musician who discovered the Library's concerts as a teenager while researching a term paper on classical music. And perhaps the most romantic note in patron history is the story of Harlan and Olive Harrison, who met in the Coolidge Auditorium, married, and enjoyed coming to concerts regularly for a lifetime of memorable music, always sitting in the same seats in row R, to mark their first encounter. ■

In April 2018, the Baltimore Symphony Orchestra OrchKids performed in the Great Hall and Coolidge Auditorium. The performances included an original group composition by the students that was inspired by their interaction with items from the Leonard Bernstein Collection during a January 2018 visit to the Library of Congress.

The Next Generation of Music Lovers

Supporting new generations of music lovers is an important role of Concerts from the Library of Congress. The Concert Office has a longstanding commitment to create opportunities for young and emerging musicians to learn from renowned artists and educators involved in the series. From a contemporary music masterclass with Pulitzer Prize–winning composer Richard Wernick in 2013 to saxophonist Lakecia Benjamin's educational workshop in November 2023, young musicians can access unique programs to learn from artists of many different traditions. Young people are also welcome at the concerts, where they can experience musical legends such as Spain's Jordi Savall, whose artistry has interested generations of music fans in early music.

In 2018, the Baltimore Symphony Orchestra's OrchKids program, founded by Music Director Laureate Marin Alsop, paid a series of visits to the Library. Invited by Dr. Carla Hayden—who served as director of Baltimore's Enoch Pratt Free Library immediately prior to becoming Librarian of Congress—OrchKids provides pre-K through 12 students in Baltimore with music education programs to help them develop "musical and social skills that are transferable to all areas of their lives including creativity, self-expression, and teamwork." Students were introduced to the Leonard Bernstein Collection and interacted with original music manuscripts and the Library's curators. Bernstein was one of Alsop's conducting teachers, which helped the students realize their direct connections to the musical past and brought the collection to life.

Over several months, the students developed a collaborative composition inspired by Bernstein's legacy, which they performed in the Coolidge Auditorium on Saturday, April 7, 2018, for the Library's Bernstein at 100 celebration. This approach enabled students to discover thematic and rhythmic elements of Bernstein's original music that resonated with them, and then they combined those ideas with original ideas, including improvisation. This story of students creating a new work based on historical pieces from the Library's collections perfectly encapsulates the spirit of Coolidge's original intent to inspire the American people through the musical heritage preserved at the Library.

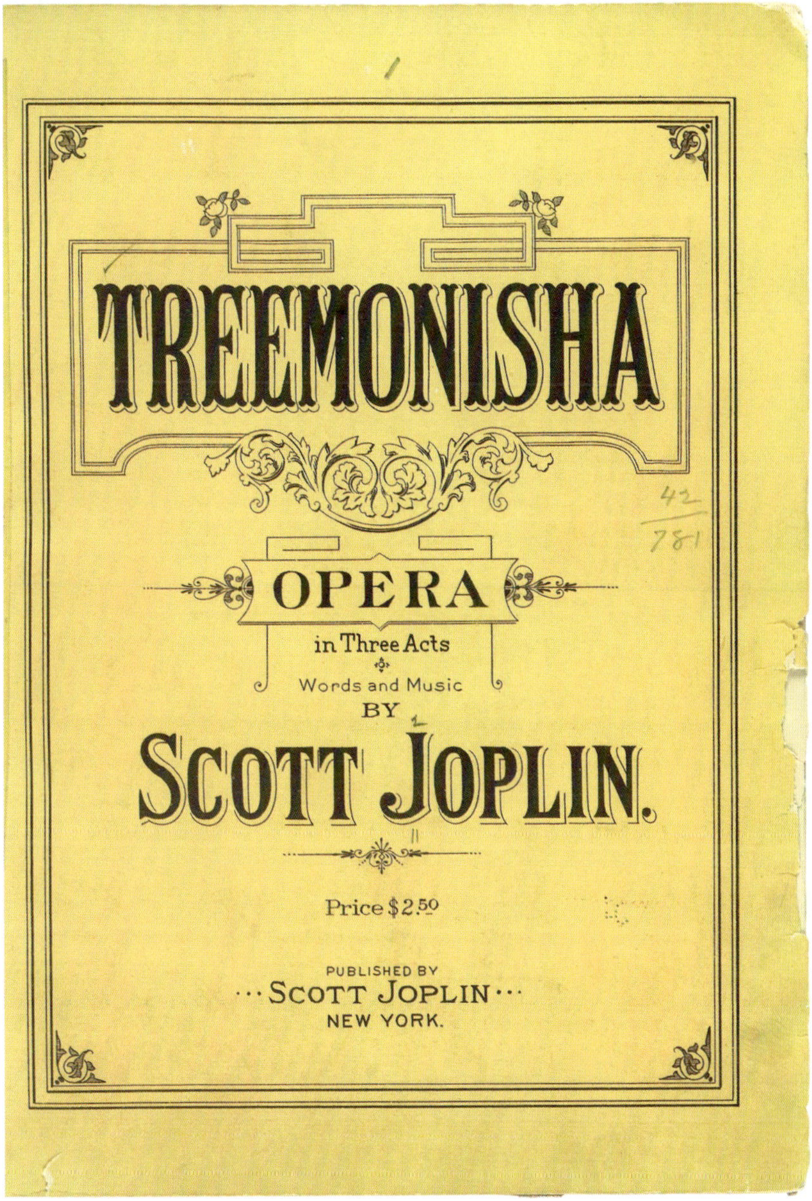

"I have heard the kids before. Every time I am overwhelmed. They are so talented. A lot of these kids live in the neighborhood I live in. And it's a pretty rough neighborhood .... The idea that these young kids have this opportunity to have their talents shown and nurtured means a lot."

—Rep. Elijah Cummings of Maryland in an interview with DC Theater Arts, April 15, 2019.

Above: *Treemonisha* by Scott Joplin, piano-vocal score, 1911. The composer famously covered the cost of printing this score so that he could deposit the work for copyright registration at the Library of Congress in his own name, even personally hand-delivering the score and his application. He never saw the opera produced during his lifetime, but it is now recognized as a formative work in the American opera canon. **Right:** In April 2018, the Baltimore Symphony Orchestra OrchKids Jazz Ensemble performed works by Jelly Roll Morton in the Coolidge Auditorium. OrchKids later returned to the Library for a project centered on African American music and Scott Joplin's opera *Treemonisha* (1911).

NATIONAL RECORDING REGISTRY
LIBRARY
"ALL I WANT FOR CHRISTMAS IS YOU"
1994
MARIAH CAREY
Mariah Carey
Artist
CERTIFIED APRIL, 2023

Music in the Community

During the 2016-2025 tenure of fourteenth Librarian of Librarian of Congress Dr. Carla Hayden, the Music Division, National Audio-Visual Conservation Center, Signature Programs Office, and American Folklife Center began collaborations with the Library's Center for Literacy, Learning, and Engagement to extend music programming to a broader audience of local concertgoers and national and international visitors. The Music Division, in partnership with Washington Performing Arts, launched Summer Concerts on the Lawn in 2018 to showcase local musicians, dancers, and performers in conjunction with the Summer Movies on the Lawn series, ranging from brass ensemble DuPont Brass to contemporary dancer Crazy Legz, "The King of Beat Ya Feet" dance. In 2022, Live! At the Library, a weekly open house event in the Thomas Jefferson Building, launched with extended visitor hours for the public to enjoy happy hour while immersing themselves in exhibits, collections, and programs, including concert series performances and informal Café Concerts that take place in open spaces throughout the Jefferson Building.

Opposite page: Librarian of Congress Carla Hayden and Santa Claus present pop superstar Mariah Carey with a framed certificate honoring the induction of her hit song "All I Want for Christmas Is You" into the 2023 Library of Congress National Recording Registry during Live! at the Library, December 14, 2023.

Below: Jerrilynn Patton, known professionally as "Jlin," appeared during Live! At the Library on Thursday, May 15, 2025. The performance included the world premiere of her Library of Congress Anne Adlum Hull and William Remsen Strickland Fund commissions *Veyari (Sanctum Aeternum)* (2025) and *Dance with my Favorite Opponent* (2025). These works were the first Library of Congress commissions for DJ and electronic dance music.

Scene 3: Dance and Theater

The role of music in dance and theater has been explored throughout the history of Concerts from the Library of Congress. Leading American and international dancers, choreographers, designers, musical theater creators, and directors have appeared for special engagements. The inclusion of dance and theater in the concert series is rooted in the collections. Throughout the twentieth century, the Music Division added collecting programs for contemporary and American dance, musical theater, and American theater. With a focus on creators, performance troupes, and performers who have been hugely influential on American culture— such as American Ballet Theater, Alvin Ailey, Katherine Dunham, Richard Rodgers, Oscar Hammerstein II, Cole Porter, and Jeanine Tesori—the collections and related events attract a wide range of researchers and visitors to the Library. Like with the series' concerts, dance and theater events focus on supporting the development of new works, reinterpretations of historically significant works, and rediscoveries of works that have been preserved in the collection that can be uniquely experienced at the Library. There is also a rich history in the twenty-first century of creating opportunities for communities to gather at the Library to participate in popular dance forms including salsa, bachata, disco, and electronic dance music in social dance workshops and the Live! At the Library series.

Opposite page: PeiJu Chien-Pott of the Martha Graham Dance Company performs as the sorceress Medea in *Cave of the Heart*, April 1, 2016, during the Martha Graham at the Library Festival. Choreography and costumes by Martha Graham, music by Samuel Barber, set by Isamu Noguchi.

Moving to the Beat: Modern Dance at the Library

Concerts from the Library of Congress first featured dance on April 27–29, 1928, with a program conceived and directed by Russian American dancer and choreographer Adolph Bolm, who was one of the Ballets Russes' leading men. The centerpiece of the inaugural dance performances was the US premiere of Igor Stravinsky's *Apollon Musagète*, commissioned by the Elizabeth Sprague Coolidge Foundation. The commissioning and presentation of Stravinsky's music in the nation's capital was a major event at the time—the explosive premiere of his *Le sacre du printemps* (*The Rite of Spring*, 1913) took place fifteen years earlier in Paris with the Ballets Russes. Additional Bolm works featured on the programs were *Pavane*, set to Maurice Ravel's work *Pavane pour une infante défunte* (1899), *Arlecchinata* (1928) with music by Jean-Joseph Cassanea de Mondonville, and *Alt-Wien: A "Fasching" Episode* (1928) with music by Beethoven. Members of the Philadelphia Orchestra accompanied the dancers under the baton of Hans Kindler, who went on to establish the National Symphony Orchestra in 1931. From this first presentation of dance and the inclusion of the Stravinsky commission, Elizabeth Sprague Coolidge's musical vision was seen to extend to other art forms.

Following the Great Depression and lean budgetary years, dance performances—which are typically more resource intensive to present than concerts—returned to the series with a splash in 1944, with the landmark collaboration between Coolidge, the Library, and dancer and choreographer Martha Graham. The Library periodically commissioned works for the Martha Graham Dance Company; this relationship, and other presentations of contemporary dance, has connected the Washington, DC, arts community with many leading dancers, choreographers, and designers, despite the modest size of the Coolidge Auditorium.

Left: Holograph manuscript piano score of Igor Stravinsky's *Apollon Musagète* (1927).

Above: Drawing of Igor Stravinsky by Miguel Covarrubias. Ink brush over graphite with opaque white. Featured in "Prodigious figures in the world of music," *Vanity Fair*, October 1925.

Opposite page: (Top) During the series' centennial celebration, the series presented dance works featuring members of the Erick Hawkins Dance Company and the Daedalus Quartet, set to music by Lucia Dlugoszewski (June 3, 2025). (Bottom) Signed program from the April 23, 1931, concert entitled "A Program of Organ and Chamber Music with stage action devised and directed by Irene Lewisohn." This concert illustrates how the series showcases contemporary dance set to mixed chamber music and solo instrumental repertoire.

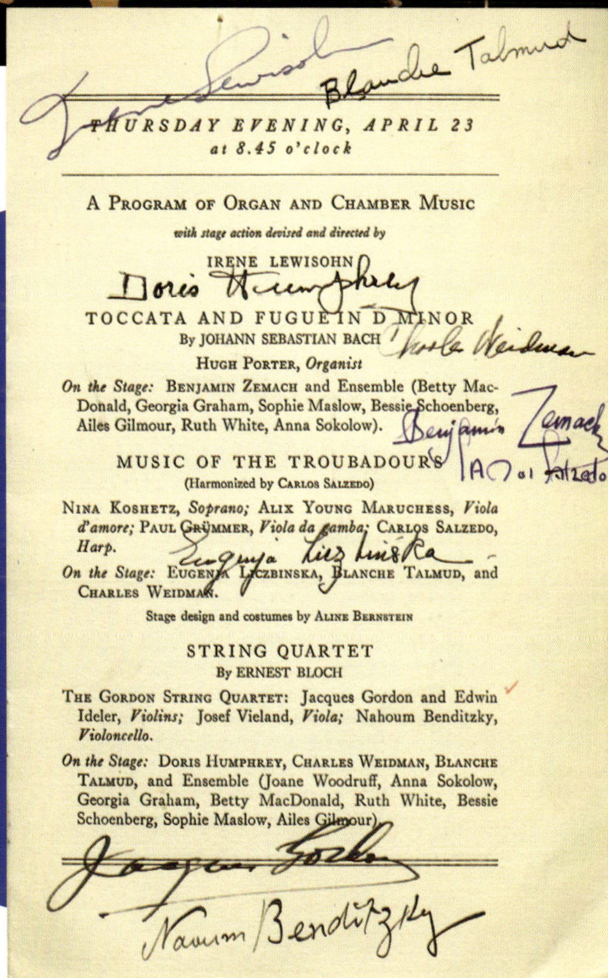

THURSDAY EVENING, APRIL 23
at 8.45 o'clock

A Program of Organ and Chamber Music
with stage action devised and directed by
IRENE LEWISOHN

TOCCATA AND FUGUE IN D MINOR
By JOHANN SEBASTIAN BACH
Hugh Porter, *Organist*

On the Stage: Benjamin Zemach and Ensemble (Betty MacDonald, Georgia Graham, Sophie Maslow, Bessie Schoenberg, Ailes Gilmour, Ruth White, Anna Sokolow).

MUSIC OF THE TROUBADOURS
(Harmonized by Carlos Salzedo)

Nina Koshetz, *Soprano;* Alix Young Maruchess, *Viola d'amore;* Paul Grümmer, *Viola da gamba;* Carlos Salzedo, *Harp.*

On the Stage: Eugenia Liczbinska, Blanche Talmud, and Charles Weidman.

Stage design and costumes by Aline Bernstein

STRING QUARTET
By ERNEST BLOCH

The Gordon String Quartet: Jacques Gordon and Edwin Ideler, *Violins;* Josef Vieland, *Viola;* Nahoum Benditzky, *Violoncello.*

On the Stage: Doris Humphrey, Charles Weidman, Blanche Talmud, and Ensemble (Joane Woodruff, Anna Sokolow, Georgia Graham, Betty MacDonald, Ruth White, Bessie Schoenberg, Sophie Maslow, Ailes Gilmour).

It was through the early collaborations with Graham's company that the Library developed relationships with several important contemporary dancers, such as Erick Hawkins, who appeared in the premiere of Aaron Copland's *Appalachian Spring* and whose papers would ultimately come to the Library, making it one of the preeminent repositories of the history of twentieth-century dance. Special dance-related collections include the papers of the Alvin Ailey Dance Foundation, American Ballet Theatre, and Lester Horton Dance Theater, and choreographers including Garth Fagan, Bronislava Njinska, Katherine Dunham, Bob Fosse and Gwen Verdon, Daniel Nagrin, and Pearl Bailey.

Production photos of Martha Graham appearing in the three major Library of Congress commissions for her eponymous dance company.

Left: Martha Graham in *Herodiade*, choreography by Martha Graham, music by Paul Hindemith, ca. 1944. *Herodiade* premiered on the same program as *Appalachian Spring* on October 30, 1944, in the Coolidge Auditorium, Library of Congress.

Middle: Martha Graham and May O'Donnell in *Appalachian Spring*, choreography by Martha Graham, music by Aaron Copland, ca. 1944.

Right: Martha Graham in *Cave of the Heart*, choreography by Martha Graham, music by Samuel Barber, ca. 1944.

Bottom: Alvin Ailey in *Hermit Songs*, 1961. Ailey created this solo dance work in dialogue with Samuel Barber's song cycle of the same title, which was commissioned by the Library of Congress.

Martha Graham and the Library

Janet Eilber, Artistic Director, Martha Graham Center of Contemporary Dance and Company

The Library of Congress holds the Martha Graham Collection, which documents the life and career of a leader in American modern dance, as a dancer, choreographer, and founder of her eponymous dance company. The collection includes more than 350,000 items, from music manuscripts and choreography notes to correspondence and business papers.

The concert series has influenced and elevated the work of the Martha Graham Dance Company since World War II. In the early 1940s, the first commissions from the Elizabeth Sprague Coolidge Foundation in the Library paired Martha Graham (1894–1991) with top composers of the day who, like the choreographer, were forging new, bold forms of expression that were born out of the American ethos. As the first government investment in American dance, the commissions offered both support and validation for Graham's often misunderstood angular and provocative modern dance style. The choreographer

The Martha Graham Dance Company performs *Appalachian Spring* in the Coolidge Auditorium, April 1, 2016, as part of the Martha Graham at the Library festival.

confirmed this in a thank you note to Coolidge, writing:

This commission of yours coming into public recognition on the moment will serve to make a seal of approval on it that nothing else could do… the public mind will accept this expression of dance as something legitimate and truly American and as an integral part of the American art scene.

The works that emerged out of those initial collaborations are now recognized as among the greatest works of mid-century modernism: *Hérodiade* (1944) created with composer Paul Hindemith; *Dark Meadow* (1946) with Carlos Chávez; and *Appalachian Spring* (1944) with Aaron Copland. Each of these creations included stunning, evocative set designs by the sculptor Isamu Noguchi, who created them only a few months after being released from an internment camp in Arizona.

This historic beginning can now be seen as a prelude to the ongoing creative activity generated by the Library and the Graham Company. Generations of Graham dancers have appeared on the Coolidge stage, dancing the same movements that were launched there decades earlier, and participating in a range of other offerings—lectures, broadcasts, and educational programs. In the years since Graham's death, commissions from the Music Division have added new dances to the company's repertory from top choreographers such as Susan Stroman and Pontus Lidberg.

Some think of a library as an archive of things past rather than as a progenitor of new art and ideas. Yet the ongoing relationship of the Martha Graham Dance Company and the Library's concert series goes well beyond creating a historical record. It is a relationship that inspires ongoing innovation, creation, and the ability of the Graham legacy to thrive, as she herself put it, "as something legitimate and truly American and as an integral part of the American art scene." ■

Top: Erick Hawkins, Elizabeth Sprague Coolidge, and Martha Graham after the premiere of *Appalachian Spring* at the Library, October 30, 1944.

Middle: Carlos Chávez, composer and conductor, March 3, 1937. Chávez was commissioned by the Elizabeth Sprague Coolidge Foundation to compose *La hija de Cólquide*, later known as *Dark Meadow*, for Martha Graham to choreograph. It was originally intended to be paired with Aaron Copland's *Appalachian Spring*, but the commission was not completed in time.

Bottom: Janet Eilber discusses the Martha Graham Dance Company's collaboration with the Library on choreographer Pontus Lidberg's *Woodland* (2016) commission, set to Irving Fine's *Notturno* (1951) for strings and harp. Whittall Pavilion, April 1, 2016.

Documenting Dance

At the turn of the twenty-first century, the Library of Congress expanded its dance collections acquisition program within the Music Division. Building on the extensive collections relating to Martha Graham and the Ballets Russes, the Library acquired the papers of major American dance companies such as American Ballet Theater, personal papers of dancers, choreographers, and designers, and the archives of organizations involved in presenting and preserving dance heritage. Dance also permeates through dozens of music-focused special collections since most major composers in the twentieth century—from Leonard Bernstein to John Adams—were composing for dance in some capacity, whether through musicals, operas, or ballets. A series of special exhibitions in the Library's Performing Arts Reading Room Gallery and online showcased these collections between 2008 and 2015, and touring versions were displayed in the Ira and Leonore Gershwin Gallery at Walt Disney Concert Hall in Los Angeles, California. Each exhibition highlighted the critical role dance has played in exporting American culture abroad and maintaining a mutual flow of talent and creativity between the United States, Europe, Russia, Latin America, and Japan.

The Performing Arts Reading Room Gallery hosted four major dance exhibitions showcasing the collections between 2008 and 2015. The concert series promoted the exhibits through performances, scholarly programs, and special events.

Celebrating Alvin Ailey

As one of the most iconic American artists of the twentieth century, Alvin Ailey had a profound impact on dance in the United States, bringing African American cultural themes to the stage through innovative choreography. The archive of his life's work entered the Library's collections in 2006. Librarian of Congress Dr. James H. Billington, US Senator Hillary Rodham Clinton (New York), Congressman Jerrold Nadler (New York), and Judith Jamison, Alvin Ailey Dance Theater artistic director, presided over the event, which marked the Library's first acquisition from a predominantly Black international touring dance company. The highlight of the program was a featured performance by Alvin Ailey Dance Theater members Renee Robinson, Matthew Rushing, and Dwana Adiaha Smallwood, who performed "Wade in the Water" from Ailey's *Revelations* (1960).

"The very beauty of dance helps us think more deeply about our shared human experience."

—Senator Hillary Rodham Clinton on the acquisition of the Alvin Ailey Dance Foundation Archive at the Library of Congress, February 8, 2006

Opposite page: Dwight Rhoden, Desmond Richardson, and Aubrey Lynch II performing Alvin Ailey's *Revelations*, 1991.

This page: Ilana Ruth Cohen performs *Ballad in a Popular Style* (2023), by Eleanor Bunker and Samantha Géracht (after Anna Sokolow), music by Alex North/Kevin Kaska, Coolidge Auditorium, January 26, 2024.

Reconstructing Dance

The Library's relationship with dance collections and classical and modern Western dance presentations reflects the cyclical nature of creating and performing repertoire. A contemporary example is the January 2024 presentation of "Anna Sokolow and the Reimagined Roots of Anti-fascist Dance," a lecture and performance that explored the restoration of "early activist dances" of American choreographer Anna Sokolow, who was a principal dancer in the Martha Graham Dance Company before branching out on her own. Music Division curators connected Sokolow Theatre/Dance Ensemble Artistic Director Samantha Géracht with music manuscripts by Sokolow collaborator Alex North in the division's collections. With access to this material, the Sokolow Theatre/Dance Ensemble reimagined several of Sokolow's works for performance at the Library, based solely on knowledge of Sokolow's technique and the documentary evidence in the music manuscripts, photographs, and videos.

Popular Dance

While dance presentations in the concert series have historically focused on twentieth- and twenty-first century contemporary dance, popular American dance styles have been featured at various other Library of Congress events. The Gershwin Prize for Popular Song concerts have featured performances by tap dancer Savion Glover, the cast of Gloria and Emilio Estefan's musical *On Your Feet!* (2015), and the cast of Billy Joel's *Movin' Out* (2002) musical with choreography by Twyla Tharp. The Summer Concerts on the Lawn series, established in 2018, has featured Washington, DC–based artist Crazy Legz and Bachata workshops and social dances with Julissa Cruz and DJ Hercules. These high-energy events draw hundreds of participants and viewers and were notable for bringing contemporary popular art forms into the spotlight in nontraditional spaces of the northwest lawn and mezzanine of the Thomas Jefferson Building.

The American Folklife Center's Homegrown Concerts, which are supported by the Music Division's Concert Office staff, regularly feature traditional dance performances, from Afro-Peruvian dance with Negrura Peruana to Unukupukupu, a hula halau (a traditional Hawaiian performance troupe) from Hawai'i Community College. Since so much traditional folk music is for dance, the Homegrown series is an outstanding platform for showcasing the music of popular and social dance forms.

Top: Tap dancer Savion Glover performs at the Library of Congress Gershwin Prize for Popular Song honoring Tony Bennett, DAR Constitution Hall, Washington, DC, November 15, 2017. **Bottom:** The cast of *Movin' Out* (2002) performs at the Library of Congress Gershwin Prize for Popular Song honoring Billy Joel, November 19, 2014, DAR Constitution Hall, Washington, DC.

Top, left: Phil Wiggins (right), playing harmonica with John Cephas on guitar, appeared at the Library four times in the 1980s and 1990s, including for performances of traditional music for dance from the mid-Atlantic region in the American Folklife Center's Neptune Plaza Concert Series in 1981.

Top, right: Grammy-winning artist Natalie Merchant, right, who serves on the American Folklife Center's Board of Trustees, and Librarian of Congress Carla Hayden square dance during Family Day at the Library, June 15, 2024. The band is the Ken and Brad Kolodner quartet, plus Richie Stearns on banjo.

Left: The Cambodian American Heritage Dancers with Chum Ngek Ensemble performed a program of classical Khmer dance and music from the Cambodian court repertoire for the American Folklife Center's Homegrown Concerts, May 25, 2017.

Behind the Curtain: Theater at the Library

In the spring of 1939, Music Division Chief Harold Spivacke initiated correspondence with Elliott Shapiro of music publishers Shapiro, Bernstein and Co., and Ira Gershwin with the aim of acquiring some of George Gershwin's music manuscripts for the Library. Ira's response to Spivacke was favorable, though he indicated the estate of George Gershwin—he had died in 1937—would continue to retain major manuscripts for the purpose of managing his catalog. On May 16, 1939, Ira sent Spivacke an initial donation: a holograph sketch of "The Crap Shooter's Song" from *Porgy and Bess* (1935). This exchange and gift began the ongoing relationship between the Music Division and the Gershwin family, through which the family has donated the vast majority of the iconic creative duo's papers and the records of the Gershwin Trust.

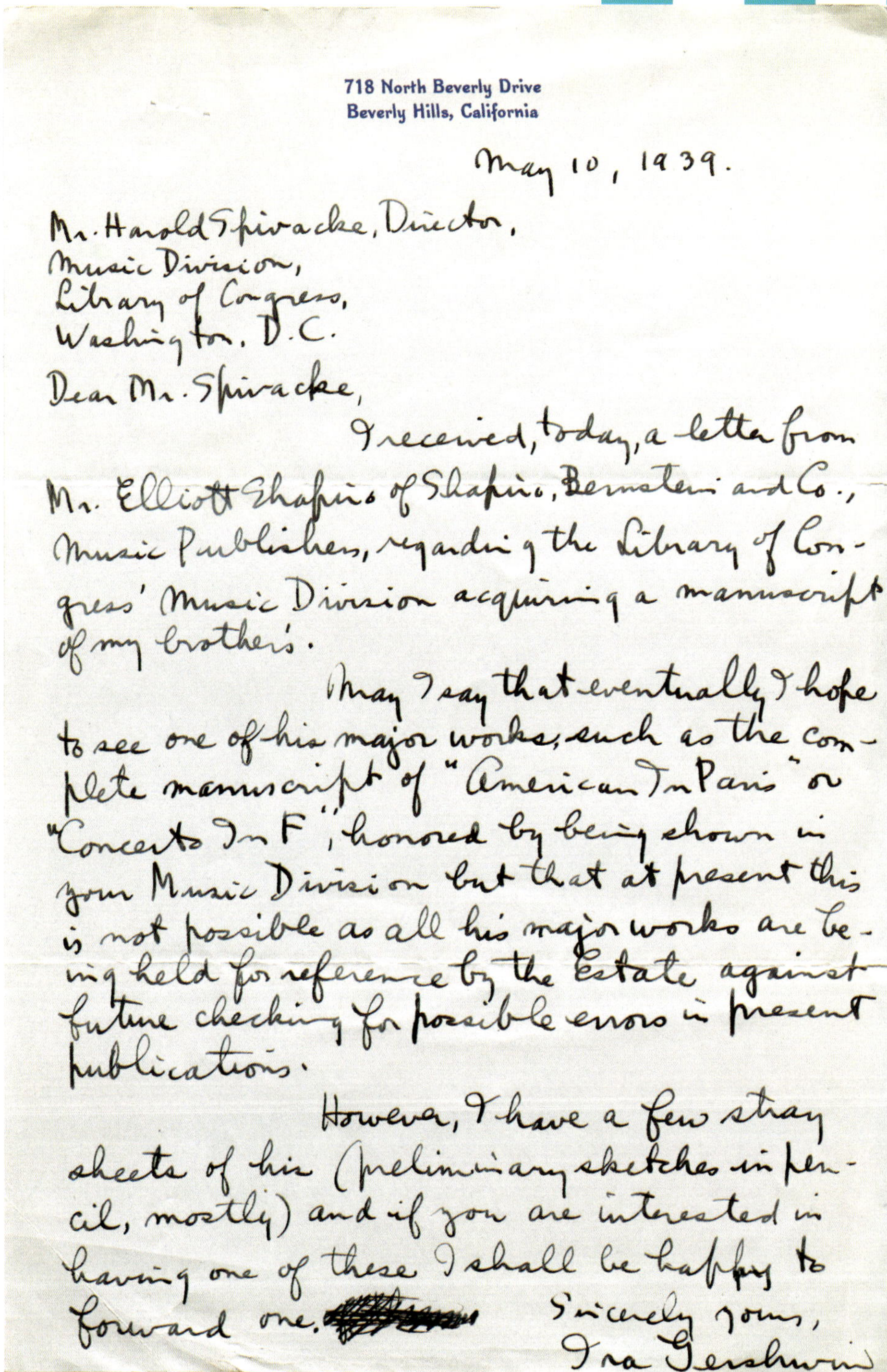
718 North Beverly Drive
Beverly Hills, California

May 10, 1939.

Mr. Harold Spivacke, Director,
Music Division,
Library of Congress,
Washington, D.C.

Dear Mr. Spivacke,

I received, today, a letter from Mr. Elliott Shapiro of Shapiro, Bernstein and Co., Music Publishers, regarding the Library of Congress' Music Division acquiring a manuscript of my brother's.

May I say that eventually I hope to see one of his major works, such as the complete manuscript of "American In Paris" or "Concerto In F", honored by being shown in your Music Division but that at present this is not possible as all his major works are being held for reference by the estate against future checking for possible errors in present publications.

However, I have a few stray sheets of his (preliminary sketches in pencil, mostly) and if you are interested in having one of these I shall be happy to forward one.

Sincerely yours,
Ira Gershwin

Letters from Ira Gershwin to Harold Spivacke discussing an initial donation of George Gershwin manuscripts to the Library of Congress, May 10, 1939.

"May I call your attention to the fact that the Music Division of the Library of Congress has the greatest collection of American manuscripts in the country? ... The Library is visited by several million people each year, many thousands of who are interested in music and expect to find things of national interest here. For this reason we naturally thought of your brother's manuscripts and were disappointed that he was not properly represented in our exhibitions or in the collection as a whole."

—Howard Spivacke to Ira Gershwin, May 12, 1939

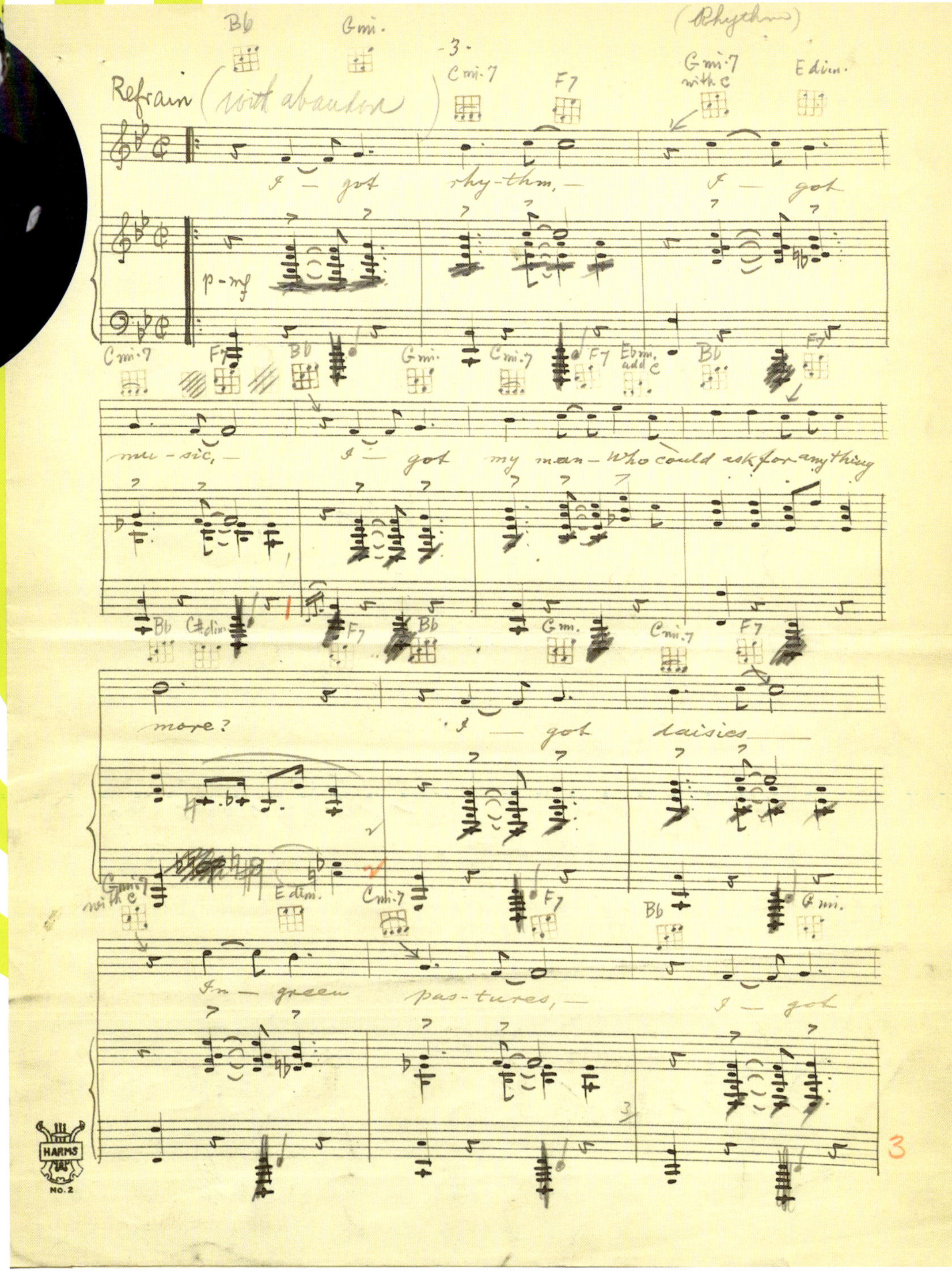

Top: George and Ira Gershwin, ca. 1920s.

Right: Excerpt from "I Got Rhythm" from *Girl Crazy* (1930) by George and Ira Gershwin, autograph manuscript piano-vocal score in a copyist's hand.

Until Ira Gershwin's initial gift, American musical theatre was primarily represented in the Performing Arts collections through the Copyright Office sheet music deposits. The arrival of original materials, between 1939 and the 1990s, of the Gershwin brothers, Richard Rodgers, Oscar Hammerstein II, Victor Herbert, Irving Berlin, Cole Porter, Frederick Loewe, and the Federal Theatre Project positioned the Library of Congress as the preeminent repository for the study of American musical theater. The concert series has provided a platform to showcase and preserve every major era in musical theater history, from Tin Pan Alley to the rock musicals of the 1990s and Jeanine Tesori's groundbreaking work in the twenty-first century.

Creating a Gershwin Recording Legacy

To mark the fiftieth anniversary of the first Gershwin manuscript donation, the Music Division presented one of the earliest major musical theater presentations in the concert series on May 22, 1989. The retrospective concert, conducted by Robert Fischer, featured performers Michael Feinstein, Christine Andreas, and Paige O'Hara. It also served to announce a partnership with Elektra/Nonesuch records to produce six recordings of the Gershwins' works for the stage and several unpublished songs, released between 1990 and 2001.

Celebrating Stephen Sondheim at 70

The most high-profile musical theater event to grace the Coolidge Auditorium stage was Stephen Sondheim's seventieth birthday concert on May 22, 2000. The blockbuster lineup featured performers Audra McDonald, Brian Stokes Mitchell, Marin Mazzie, and Debra Monk, with a twenty-five-person orchestra and a chorus of twelve. Sondheim, who had a warm friendship with Senior Music Specialist Mark Eden Horowitz, attended and eventually bequeathed his music manuscripts and correspondence to the Library of Congress. Sondheim had already donated his collection of 11,000-plus vinyl records in the 1990s.

Stephen Sondheim sitting on a sofa with his poodle Max, December 22, 1993.

"It was an extraordinary concert," said Horowitz, adding:

> *It opened with a concert version of Sondheim's (at the time very obscure) musical of Aristophanes'* The Frogs *(1974), which had been written for and was first performed in the pool at Yale. Our concert premiered new orchestrations by Jonathan Tunick. And our concert generated the first recording of the score. Nathan Lane was so taken with the show and score that he convinced Sondheim to work with him to expand it, which eventually brought it to Broadway in 2004. The second portion of the show was selected from Sondheim's "Songs I Wish I'd Written (At Least in Part)"—works by some of the great musical theater composers like Bock & Harnick, Kander & Ebb, Cy Coleman, Charles Strouse, Hugh Martin, and others.*

A Rock Musical Takes Center Stage

Jonathan Larson's Pulitzer Prize– and Tony Award–winning hit musical *RENT* (1996) took center stage for a concert celebrating the opening of the Jonathan Larson Papers at the Library of Congress for researchers on October 23, 2006. The concert was supported by the Jonathan Larson Performing Foundation and attended by the late creator's parents and sister. Anthony Rapp and Gwen Stewart, plus music director Tim Weil, of the original *RENT* Broadway cast and creative team, were featured along with performers Natascia Diaz, Randy Graff, Jeremy Kushnier, Michael McElroy, and Gwen Stewart. Larson was a mentee of Stephen Sondheim, who was previously a mentee of Oscar Hammerstein II, demonstrating the type of creative lineages represented in the Library's collections and concerts.

The Musical Worlds of Victor Herbert

Thanks to operettas such as *Babes in Toyland* (1903) and *Naughty Marietta* (1910), composer Victor Herbert was one of the fathers of American musical theater and a founder of the American Society of Composers, Authors, and Publishers (ASCAP). Elizabeth Auman and Loras John Schissel of the Music Division curated a concert entitled The Musical Worlds of Victor Herbert (December 3, 2012) to celebrate the opening of an exhibition in the Performing Arts Reading Room Gallery of the same title, which highlighted his collection at the Library. The performance featured Tony Award nominees Rebecca Luker, Ron Raines, and Aaron Lazar, opera singer Korliss Uecker, music director Bill Hicks, and Metropolitan Opera Orchestra principal cellist Jerry Grossman. Similar to the early musical theater concerts from the late 1980s and early 1990s, this program sought to bring classics from generations past to a new generation of listeners and inspire research in the collections.

Archivist Janet McKinney (left) shows Renée Elise Goldsberry and Michael McElroy, who were both in the final cast of the original Broadway production of *RENT* (1996), their headshots in the closing night playbill, during a September 29, 2023, visit to the Library. Goldsberry won a Tony Award for her performance as Angelica Schuyler in *Hamilton* (2015). McElroy performed in the Jonathan Larson concert at the Library in 2006.

Promotional flier for the 1991 production of *tick, tick...BOOM!* by Jonathan Larson at The Village Gate, New York, NY.

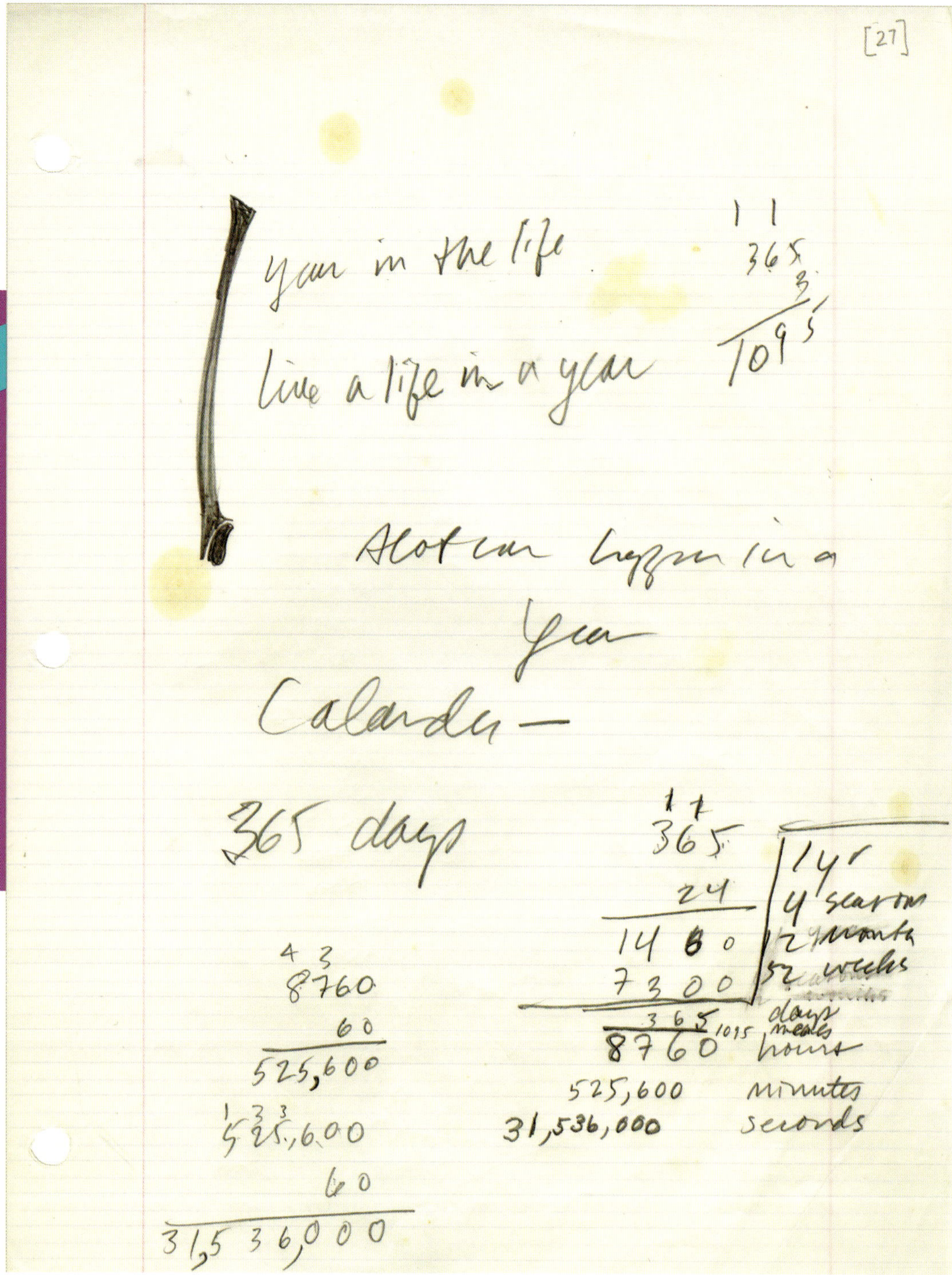
[27]

year in the life

live a life in a year

A lot can happen in a year

Calendar—

365 days

365
24
1460
730
8760

1 yr
4 seasons
12 months
52 weeks
days
hours
minutes
seconds

8760
60
525,600

525,600
60
31,536,000

525,600
31,536,000

Lyric sketches for "Seasons of Love" from *RENT* by Jonathan Larson, ca. 1989–1990. Larson calculated the number of minutes in a year, which formed an iconic lyric from the song.

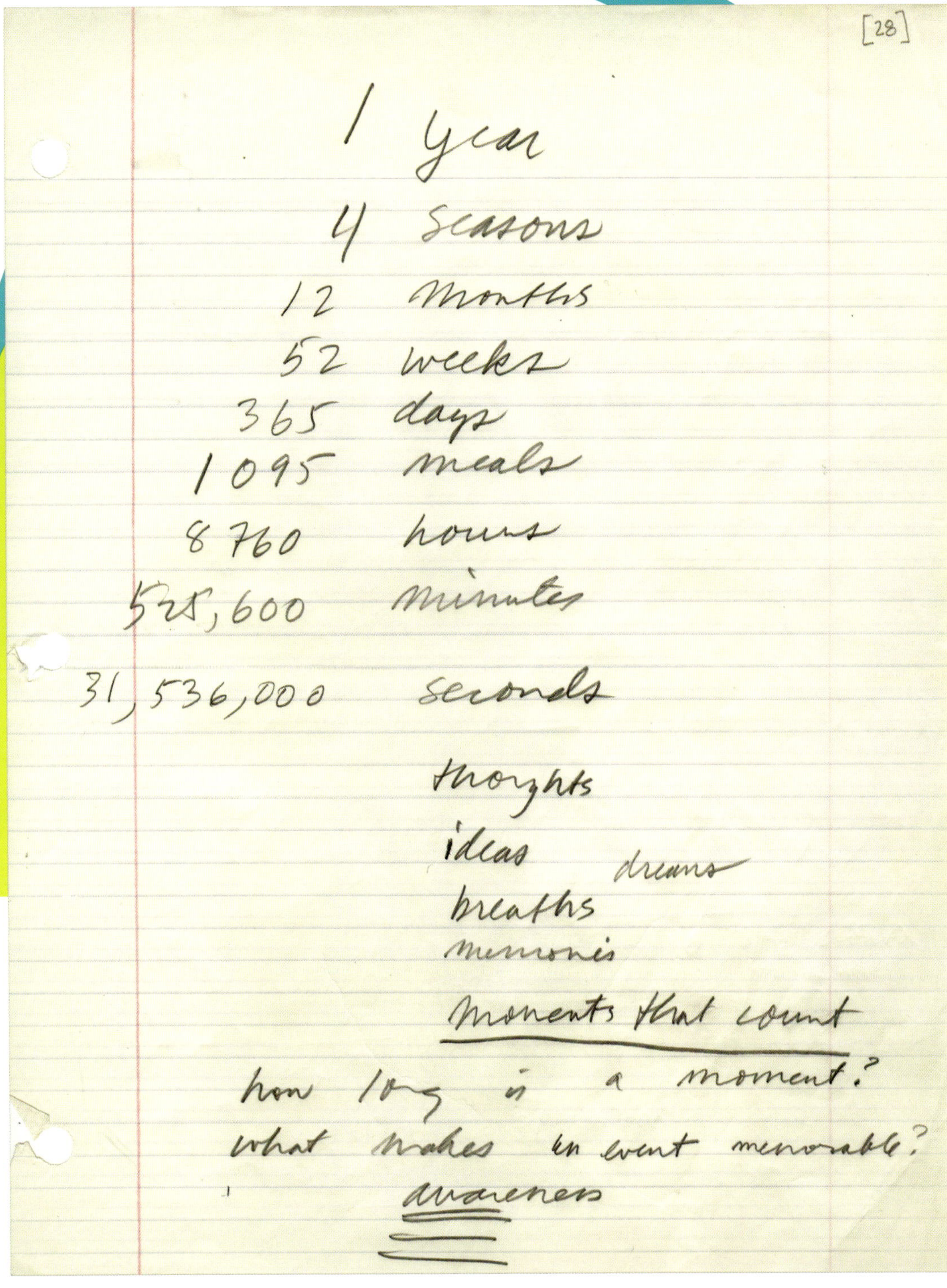
[28]

1 year

4 seasons

12 months

52 weeks

365 days

1095 meals

8760 hours

525,600 minutes

31,536,000 seconds

thoughts

ideas dreams

breaths

memories

moments that count

how long is a moment?

what makes an event memorable?

awareness

Top: Aaron Lazar and Rebecca Luker perform "Give Your Heart in June-Time" from Victor Herbert's *Sky High* (1925), lyrics by Harold Atteridge, in The Musical Worlds of Victor Herbert concert, accompanied by music director Bill Hicks, December 3, 2012.

Bottom: Victor Herbert (left), Irving Berlin (center), and John Phillip Sousa (right), April 17, 1924, Cannon House Office Building, Washington, DC.

A New Generation of Broadway Creators

Between 2014 and 2023, several contemporary Broadway creators were featured in the concert series, including Jeanine Tesori (*Fun Home*, 2013, *Thoroughly Modern Millie*, 2000), David Yazbek (*The Band's Visit*, 2016, *Dirty Rotten Scoundrels*, 2004, *The Full Monty*, 2000), and Steven Lutvak (*A Gentleman's Guide to Love and Murder*, 2012), who appeared together on October 1, 2014, and Jason Robert Brown (*The Bridges of Madison County*, 2014, *The Last Five Years*, 2001, *Parade*, 1998), who appeared with Tony-nominated artist Shoshana Bean on December 9, 2016. Justin Paul and Benj Pasek (*La La Land*, 2016, and *Dear Evan Hansen*, 2015) performed for the 2023 ASCAP/ Library of Congress We Write the Songs concert, connecting the Millennial and Gen Z audiences who grew up with these shows to the broader heritage of musical theater at the Library. Collectively, these creators are responsible for some of the most successful Broadway shows of the first quarter of the twenty-first century.

Top: Shoshana Bean, who appeared as Elphaba in *Wicked* on Broadway, holding holding a holograph manuscript score of "For Good" from Stephen Schwartz's score, February 19, 2025.

Middle: Jeanine Tesori performs her own music in the Coolidge Auditorium, October 17, 2014.

Bottom: Broadway, film, and television star Audra McDonald performed an exclusive recital in February 2014 for the concert series soon after her hit run as Bess in *The Gershwins' Porgy and Bess* on Broadway in 2012. McDonald visited the *Here to Stay: The Legacy of George and Ira Gershwin* exhibition in the Gershwin Gallery of the Thomas Jefferson Building. Her concert connects her to the Gershwin legacy at the Library as one of the major interpreters of the role of Bess.

Way Down in *Hadestown*

The concert series often presents educational programs that highlight the intersection of the collections with live performance. On October 17, 2023, the cast and company of *Hadestown* (2019) by Anaïs Mitchell performed selections from the Tony Award–winning musical, followed by a post-show conversation moderated by Peter Marks of *The Washington Post*. The event was hosted by Librarian Carla Hayden and attended by Washington, DC, area middle and high school students and arts educators. Mitchell gave a cameo performance and donated several archival items from the show's creation to the Library, including handwritten lyric sketches and voice memos of music and lyric sketches. The show's producers donated a 1950 Gibson TG50 tenor guitar used by the character Orpheus (played by Reeve Carney) during the pre-Broadway, London run of the show. Carney was joined by Solea Pfeiffer, Betty Who, and Lillias White—all then-members of the Broadway cast—for the performance.

The Visual Art of Theater

The Music Division's theater special collections include the papers of playwrights, designers, producers, and impresarios, from Florence Klotz's costume design drawings for *A Little Night Music* (1973) and *Kiss of the Spider Woman* (1992) and Oliver Smith's scenic designs for Broadway productions such as *On the Town* (1945) and *Guys and Dolls* (1950), to Neil Simon's scripts for *The Odd Couple* (1964) and *Plaza Suite* (1969). These collections provide ample opportunities for scholars and artists to engage with the history of theater for reimagination and reinterpretation. Imagery from these collections—like the Tony Walton costumes for *The Wiz* (1978)—are iconic in twentieth-century American performing arts history.

Opposite page, top: Scenic design depicting the outside of Professor Higgins' House from *My Fair Lady* by Oliver Smith, 1976, for revival production at St. James Theatre, New York, NY.

Opposite page, bottom: Pop singer Betty Who appears as Persephone with the *Hadestown* cast and company, Coolidge Auditorium, October 17, 2023.

This page: Tony Walton's costume design for Dorothy, played by Diana Ross, in the 1978 film *The Wiz*.

Ted Van Griethuysen and Steve Nixon in Samuel Beckett's *Ohio Impromptu* (1980), directed by Joy Zinoman, March 7, 2012, Coolidge Auditorium.

Expanding the Repertoire

The Music Division's commissioning funds have supported multidisciplinary stage works throughout its history, from Benjamin Britten's *Peter Grimes* (1945), a Koussevitzky Music Foundation Commission, to a musical adaptation of Samuel Beckett's *Ohio Impromptu* (1981), which was presented as the inaugural concert of the Dina Koston and Roger Shapiro Fund for New Music in the Library on March 7, 2012. Works by Koston, Chester Biscardi, Ferruccio Busoni, David Claman, and Frank Brickle filled out the season, along with the world premiere of Mario Davidovsky's *Ladino Songs* for voice and ensemble (2011), commissioned by the Koston and Shapiro Fund. The performance of *Ohio Impromptu* at the Library represented an important development stage for the work, which later transferred to off-Broadway in an expanded version the same year as the performance at the Library. While the concert series has traditionally focused its commissioning program on music and dance works, there have been occasional instances—like the *Ohio Impromptu* project—when collections connections have motivated the support of individual special projects.

Brazilian jazz artist Eliane Elias appeared in the Coolidge Auditorium on October 13, 2023.

The Need to Always Evolve

Throughout its first hundred years, the scope and artistic breadth of Concerts from the Library of Congress' programming has evolved, such as with the inclusion of regular jazz concerts in the twenty-first century. In honoring the true definition of chamber music, as *musica da camera*, or, music of the chamber, the Library's series now presents a range of genres, with a classical and contemporary chamber music core, that is ideally suited to an intimate acoustic. As Elizabeth Sprague Coolidge noted in her Founder's Day remarks in 1950,

> *I have often felt that my work for Chamber Music has shaped my own destiny quite as truly as I have attempted to guide its course. It has given my life a significance which had not, before, been revealed to me. And, in this interchange of giving and receiving, the Library of Congress has been a supreme factor of help and inspiration—not only by responding to and developing my intentions, but by creating and supporting new ones."*

She understood the need to always evolve, to both persevere and augment, and the essential role of the audience and creative partners in the pursuit of artistic excellence. Concerts from the Library of Congress is not beholden to just one acoustically superlative space, but rather to the spirit of the institution that fosters interaction at the crossroads of knowledge and inspiration.

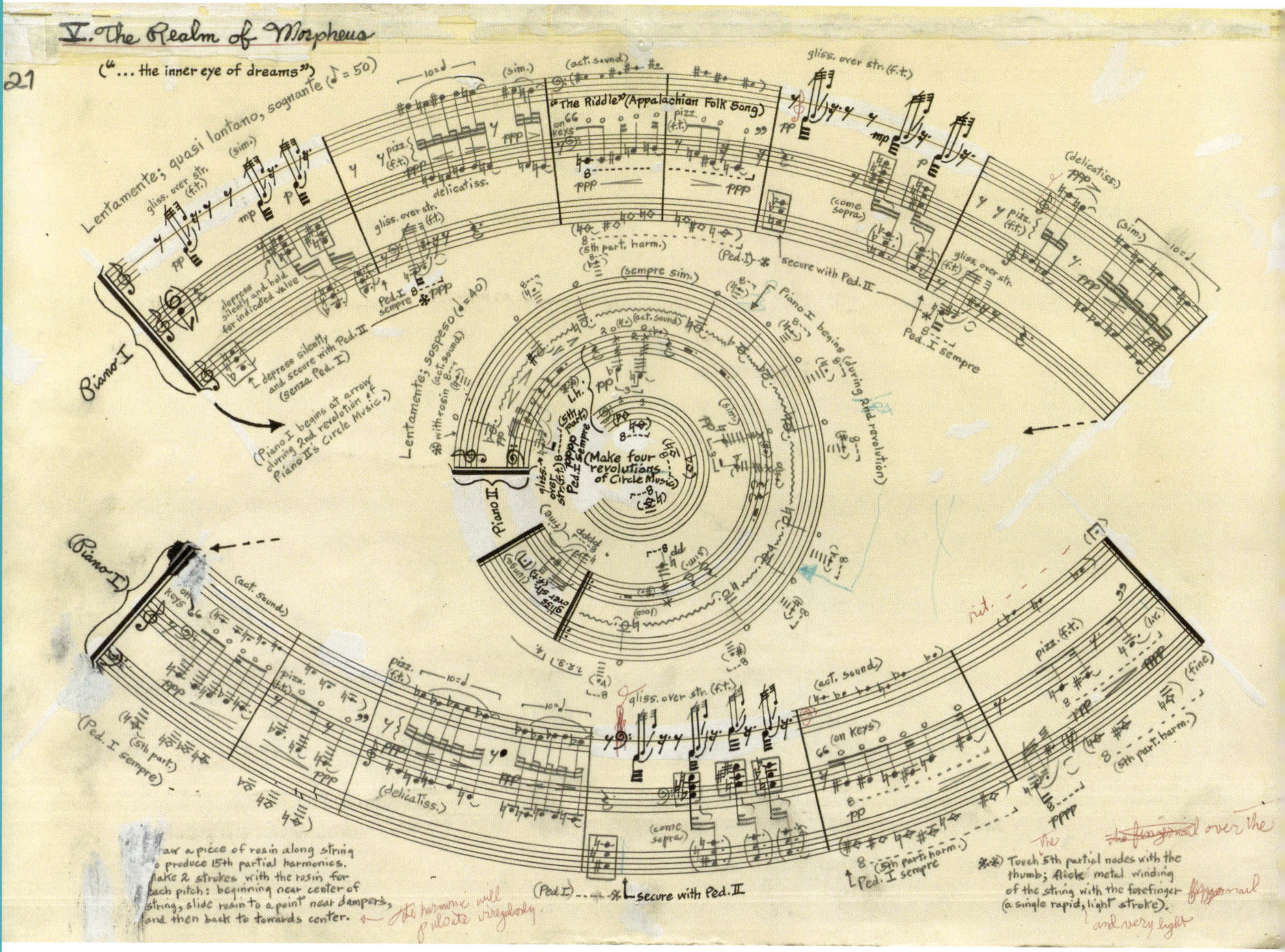

George Crumb, *Zeitgeist*, fifth movement, *The Realm of Morpheus*, 1987, holograph manuscript. *The Realm of Morpheus* is one of Crumb's compelling score visualizations, this one in the shape of an eye. He made practical, straight-line versions of the music at the end of the score to facilitate performance. Crumb's manuscript, which resembles an all-seeing eye and conjures the dreamy Realm of Morpheus, is a fitting symbol for the future of the ever-evolving concert series.

Epilogue

"An unparalleled establishment for the propagation of art and learning."

On April 5, 1929, dignitaries and Library of Congress officials gathered in the Coolidge Auditorium to celebrate the thirtieth anniversary of Librarian Herbert Putnam's appointment to lead the institution. Music Division Chief Carl Engel delivered remarks to commemorate the legacy he envisioned for the Library's concert series, made possible under Putnam's support and gesturing to the significant musical accomplishments that would forever be associated with both of their tenures. The remarkable speech Engel delivered, "Concert A.D. 2025 in the Library of Congress," imagined an occasion 100 years following the inauguration of the concert series in which the future chief recounts the impacts of a century of music-making at the nation's library. The commentary sought to shape the collective joint musical legacy of Engel, Putnam, and Elizabeth Sprague Coolidge, while anticipating changes in society and predicting ways to ensure that the traditions of chamber music always have a home at the Library alongside modern music, which "acquired new sonority, new purity, new beauty." Engel encapsulated the imagined impact of the first hundred years of the concert series in his description of the Library's role in preserving the living musical traditions represented in its collections.

> ***"With the aid of forward-looking and generous citizens, our Government has been enabled to rear an unparalleled establishment for the propagation of learning."***
>
> – Engel in "Concert A.D. 2025 in the Library of Congress"

The Library of Congress now finds itself at a similar juncture in its musical history. Under the leadership of Dr. Carla Hayden, the Library embraced a vision that affirms how America's strength lies in its diversity of people and cultures. As the Library's original and flagship concert series, Concerts from the Library of Congress will continue to serve as an essential national platform for the celebration of cultural traditions and contemporary creativity. Coolidge and Engel's objective of creating a national home for the advancement of chamber music continues to be realized; however, they also believed in the importance of exposing audiences to other genres and art forms that contribute to the intellectual and cultural life of America.

In the 1920s and 1930s, Coolidge and Engel expressed this programming philosophy by ensuring vocal music and dance were represented in the series, in addition to instrumental chamber music. In the ensuing decades, Music Division chiefs worked to reflect the expanding scope of the Division's special collections in the series, from a focus on Western classical music and American popular song to include contemporary genres that developed in the twentieth and twenty-first centuries, providing a lens into how music facilitates cross-cultural understanding within both the United States and the broader global cultural community. Contemporary dance, American musical theater, jazz, electronic music, and country music are among the genres and art forms that have found a place in the concert series.

The underlying and central commitment to the promotion of chamber music is embedded in the evolution of the series, given that programming must align with Library's collections of music manuscripts and special collections. Engel recognized from the beginning that the longevity of Concerts from the Library of Congress would be entirely dependent on the concert program being fully embedded in the collection's development.

Over the next one hundred years, the Concerts from the Library of Congress will continue to engage generations of Americans through the Library's performing arts collections. Following the blueprint provided by Coolidge, Engel, and Putnam, the series will continue to support creativity and community in the Coolidge Auditorium and through digital and broadcast engagement as technology evolves. The traditions of Western classical and American music will be enjoyed, reinterpreted, and reexamined as new technologies, performance practices, genres, and new cultural contexts emerge.

The thousands of artists who have shared their perspectives on repertoire both old and new have helped countless Americans and international visitors find community both in the Coolidge Auditorium and around the world through radio broadcasts and digital media. Concerts from the Library of Congress is an American treasure that exists through the generous philanthropy of supporters who have embraced Coolidge's vision for democratizing access to the music that can bring us together. It represents the same American spirit imbued in *Appalachian Spring*, a hope for a future in which our shared experiences are stronger than our differences. In the words of Engel, "The Elizabeth Sprague Coolidge Foundation has borne rich fruit; it has upheld musical standards and furthered musical advancement."

Acknowledgements

The authors extend their appreciation to former Music Division Chief Susan H. Vita and former Assistant Chief Jan Lauridsen for their distinguished leadership of the Concert Office over many years, as well as contributors Janet Eilber, David Harrington, and Nicholas Kitchen, and Music Division contributors Anne E. McLean, Kate Rivers, Loras John Schissel, Paul Allen Sommerfeld, and Carol Lynn Ward-Bamford. In addition, the authors gratefully acknowledge the assistance of colleagues throughout the Library who have lent their time and support to this project: fourteenth Librarian of Congress Carla Hayden, Acting Librarian of Congress Robert R. Newlen; Becky Clark, Hannah Freece, Aimee Hess, Zach Klitzman, and Susan Reyburn (Publishing Office); Roswell Encina and Ryan Ramsey (Office of the Librarian); Deputy Librarian of Congress Robin Dale; Associate Librarian of Congress for Researcher and Collection Services Hannah Sommers; Director of the Special Collections Directorate Jennifer Meehan; Shawn Miller (Office of Communications); Glenn Ricci and Joon Yi (Multimedia Group) and Joel Kaufman (Duplication Services). The authors also extend thanks to their families, especially Nicholas' husband Christopher Neuhaus, and David's wife Alison Lowell and their daughters Adelaide and Penelope.

This publication is made possible in part by the Verna and Irving Fine Endowment in the Library of Congress.

The VERNA AND IRVING FINE ENDOWMENT in the Library of Congress was established in 2000 through a generous bequest of Verna Rudnick Fine (1920–99) as a memorial to her husband, the distinguished American composer and educator Irving Gifford Fine (1914–62). A member of the "Boston School" of composers, Irving Fine served on the music faculty at Harvard from 1939 to 1950, where he become a close associate of Aaron Copland, Igor Stravinsky, Serge Koussevitzky, and Leonard Bernstein. Fine experimented with many styles throughout his career, including serialism, romantic expressivity, and neoclassicism; Copland praised Fine's music for its "keenly conceived sonorities" and "elegance," while Virgil Thompson cited its "unusual melodic grace." During Fine's twelve years as an educator, mentor, and administrator at Brandeis University, he founded and chaired its School of Creative Arts, brought Bernstein and Copland to the faculty of the young institution, and helped establish it as an internationally recognized breeding ground for artistic talent. After the death of her husband, Verna Fine embarked on a career as an artist management consultant in New York City, earning a highly respected reputation as a champion and advocate for American composers.

Opposite page: Argentine rock artist Fito Páez reflecting on his experience playing George Gershwin's piano during a tour of the Library, April 11, 2025.

Gift and Trust Funds that Support the Concert Series

1926: Elizabeth Sprague Coolidge Foundation

1933: The Nicholas Longworth Foundation

1936: Gertrude Clarke Whittall Foundation

1942: Friends of Music in the Library of Congress Fund [Trust Fund]

1945: Louis C. Elson Memorial Fund

1949: The Serge Koussevitzky Music Foundation

1958: Friends of Music [Gift Fund]

1967: Norman P. Scala Memorial Fund

1969: Katie and Walter Louchheim Fund

1969: Leonora Jackson McKim Fund

1978: Da Capo Fund

1980: Mae and Irving Jurow Fund

1980: Boris and Sonya Kroyt Memorial Fund

1984: Kindler Foundation Trust Fund

1985: Isenbergh Clarinet Fund

1990: William and Adeline Croft Memorial Fund

1990: Carolyn Royall Just Fund

1990: Rose and Monroe Vincent Fund

1992: Ira and Leonore Gershwin Fund

1992: Anne Adlum Hull and William Remsen Strickland Fund

1994: Julian E. Berla and Freda Hauptman Berla Fund

1995: The Karl B. Schmid Memorial Fund

1998: The Robert Mann Trust Fund for Chamber Music

2000: Verna and Irving Fine Endowment

2002: Judith Lieber Tokel and George Sonneborn Fund

2006: Dance Heritage Gift Fund

2006: The Wanda Landowska/Restout Memorial Fund

2010: Dina Koston and Roger Shapiro Fund for New Music

2018: Elmer Cerin—Chamber Music Concerts [Closed 2024]

2018: Sally Hart and Bennett Tarlton McCallum Fund

2021: Elinor D. Sosne Fund for Music

2024: William I. Bandas Trust Fund

2024: St. Nicholas Fund

Selected Bibliography & Further Resources

Barr, Cyrilla. *The Coolidge Legacy*. Library of Congress, 1997. https://lccn.loc.gov/97019865.

Barr, Cyrilla. *Elizabeth Sprague Coolidge: American Patron of Music*. Schirmer Books, 1998.

Bynog, David. "The 1919 Berkshire Festival Competition: A Momentous Weekend in the Viola's History." Violinist.com, August 22, 2019. https://www.violinist.com/blog/dbynog/20198/27888/.

Fishburn, Whitney M. "When BSO's OrchKids Show Up, Good Things Happen." *DC Theater Arts*, April 15, 2019. https://DCtheaterarts.org/2019/04/15/bso-orchkids.

Library of Congress. *Chamber Music: The Life and Legacy of Elizabeth Sprague Coolidge*. Digital exhibition, 2015–16. https://www.loc.gov/exhibits/elizabeth-sprague-coolidge-chamber-music/index.html.

Locke, Ralph P., and Barr, Cyrilla, eds. *Cultivating Music in America: Women Patrons and Activists Since 1860*. University of California Press, 1997.

South Mountain Concerts. "About South Mountain Concerts," n.d. http://www.southmountainconcerts.org/about.html.

Featured Special Collections

Let the People Hear It draws extensively from primary source material held in the special collections in music, theater, and dance of the Library of Congress Music Division. Finding aids for these featured collections are available at loc.gov/rr/perform.

Alvin Ailey Dance Foundation Collection

Leonard Bernstein Collection

Elizabeth Sprague Coolidge Foundation Collection

Irving Fine Collection

George and Ira Gershwin Collection

Martha Graham Collection

Serge Koussevitzky Archive

Jonathan Larson Papers

Koussevitzky Music Foundation Collection

Library of Congress Friends of Music Records

Leonora Jackson McKim Papers

Max Roach Papers

McKim Fund Collection

Tony Walton Theatrical Designs and Notebooks

Gertrude Clarke Whittall Foundation Collection

Entrance doors to the Coolidge Auditorium, the main home of the Library's concert series.

Image Credits

All images are from the Library of Congress unless otherwise noted. If no photographer is listed, the photographer is unknown. Images from the Prints and Photographs Division (P&P) can be found online by searching at loc.gov/pictures using the reproduction number provided. Images labeled "MMG" are made by the Library's Multimedia Group from archival videos of performances and other events. Users can search for and view these videos at loc.gov using the Library of Congress Control Number (LCCN) provided below. Many other concerts and events can be viewed at loc.gov/collections/event-videos/and on the Library of Congress YouTube channel.

The following abbreviations are used throughout the Image Credits:

ESCFC: Elizabeth Sprague Coolidge Foundation Collection

GCWFC: Gertrude Clarke Whittall Foundation Collection

MD: Music Division

MMG: Multimedia Group

MSS: Manuscript Division

OC: Office of Communications

P&P: Prints and Photographs Division

Cover and Frontmatter

Cover, top: A member of the Martha Graham Dance Company appears in Pontus Lidberg's *Woodland*, commissioned by the Verna and Irving Fine Endowment and set to Irving Fine's *Notturno* for strings and harp, April 6, 2016. Photo by Shawn Miller, OC.

Cover, music manuscripts: (left) George Crumb, detail from *Zeigeist*, holograph sketches. George Crumb Papers, MD. Courtesy David Crumb and Faber Music. (right) Arnold Schoenberg, *Verklärte Nacht*, detail from p. 40.

Cover, bottom left: See p. 32.

Cover, bottom right: Lakecia Benjamin in performance at the Library of Congress, November 2, 2023. Photo by Edmond Joe, OC.

ii: The "Betts" violin by Antonio Stradivari, Cremona, 1704. Photo by Michael Zirkle, GCWFC, MD.

viii: Photo by Shawn Miller, OC.

x: Photo by Kimberly Powell, OC.

xii: Photo by Elaina Finkelstein, OC.

Prologue

iv–9: ESCFC, MD.

10: Brandy-Handy Photograph Collection, P&P, LC-DIG-cwpbh-03424.

11: ESCFC, MD.

Act I, Scene i

12: Photo by Shawn Miller, OC.

14–15: ESCFC, MD.

16: Created by Charles A. Platt, architect of the Coolidge. LC Archives, MSS.

17: P&P, LC-DIG-ppmsca-17487.

18: Rudolf Kolisch Collection, MD.

19: Photo by Ernest Bloch, Eric Johnson Collection of Ernest Bloch Photographs, MD.

20 (left): George Grantham Bain Collection, P&P, LC-DIG-ggbain-31660.

20 (right): Drawing by Miguel Covarrubias, P&P, LC-DIG-ppmsca-10450.

21: From the studio of Harris and Ewing, GCWFC, Music Division.

22: Public Affairs Office Photo Archive, LC Archives, MSS.

23: MD. Photo by Shawn Miller, OC.

24: Heineman Foundation Collection, MD.

25: GCWFC, MD

26: (left) Concert Office, MD.

26: (right) General Collections, MD.

27: (left) Photo by Carl Van Vechten, P&P, LC-USZ62-121305.

27: (second from left) Photo by Addison N. Scurlock, LC-USZ62-122324, P&P.

27: (second from right) Bridge 9114. Courtesy of Bridge Records.

27: (right) Photo by Carl Ven Vechten, P&P, LC-USZ62-100858.

Act I, Scene ii

28: Photo by Shawn Miller, OC.

29: GCWFC, MD.

30: League of Nations Archives, United Nations Office at Geneva Library, World Digital Library, LCCN 2021670578.

31: ESCFC, MD.

32: Public Affairs Office Photo Archive, LC Archives, Manuscript Division.

33: Correspondence Collection, MD.

35: (top) Public Affairs Office Photo Archive, LC Archives, MSS.

35: (middle) Photo by Walter H. Scott. Courtesy of the Boston Symphony Orchestra Archives.

35: (bottom) MMG, LCCN 2021689282.

36: (left) George Grantham Bain Collection, P&P, LC-DIG-ggbain-36627.

36: (right) Photo by Shawn Miller, 2022, OC.

37: Photo by Alfredo Valente, Serge Koussevitzky Archive, MD.

38: Serge Koussevitzky Archive, MD. Courtesy of Hilda Paredes, https://www.uymp.co.uk/publications/hilda-paredes-koan.

39: Serge Koussevitzky Archive, MD.

40: (top and bottom) GCWFC, MD.

42: (left) Public Affairs Office Photo Archive, LC Archives, MSS.

42: (right) ESCFC, MD.

43: George Crumb Papers, MD. Courtesy David Crumb and Faber Music.

44: MMG, LCCN 2021689936.

45: Photo by Shawn Miller, OC.

46: (top) Concert Office Program Archives, MD.

46: (bottom) Photo by Claudia Morales Garcés. Used with permission.

47: (top) Photo by Shawn Miller, OC.

47: (bottom) Photo by Michael Wilderman. Used with permission.

48: (top and bottom) Photo by Claudia Morales Garcés. Used with permission.

49: (left) Photo by William Gottlieb, William P. Gottlieb Collection, P&P. LCCN 2023868295

49: (right) Billy Strayhorn Music Manuscripts and Papers, MD. Courtesy Alyce Claerbaut, President, Billy Strayhorn Songs, Inc.

50: Photo by Michael Wilderman. Used with permission.

51: Max Roach Collection, MD. Courtesy Maxine Roach, EXE.

Act I, Scene iii

52: Photo by Shawn Miller, OC.

53: Photo by Michael Zirkle for the LC.

54: (top) Photo by Shawn Miller, OC.

54: (bottom) Photo by Tucker Densley. Used with permission.

55: MMG. https://hdl.loc.gov/loc.music/ihas.200154820.

57: (top) Photo by Frank Moore, Inc. Dayton C. Miller Collection, MD.

57: (middle) Photo by Shawn Miller, OC.

57: (bottom): MMG, LCCN 2021690659.

58: George Grantham Bain Collection, P&P, LC-DIG-ggbain-35634.

59: Artur Schnabel collection, MD. Courtesy Ann Mottier, Schnabel Music Foundation.

60: General Collections, MD.

61: Photo by Michael Zirkle, GCWFC, MD.

62: Photo by John Waddle. Courtesy of the Oberlin Violinmaker's Workshop.

64: Photo by Shawn Miller, OC.

65: (left) Concert Office Program Archives, MD.

65: (right) MMG, 2021688056.

66: (left) MD, Courtesy of George Izenour Associates.

66: (middle and right) Public Affairs Office Photo Archive, LC Archives, Manuscript Division.

67: MMG, LCCN 2024696945.

Act II, scene i

68: Photo by Shawn Miller, OC.

70: Photo by Amanda K. Reynolds, OC

71: Concert Office Records, MD.

72: ESCFC, MD.

73: MMG, LCCN 2024697181.

74: MMG, LCCN 2024697732.

75: Bridge 9156 (top) and 9046 (middle). Courtesy of Bridge Records.

75: (bottom) Photo by MSgt Rachel Ghadiali, "The Presidents Own" United States Marine Band.

76: Photo by Shawn Miller, OC.

77: Haris & Ewing, MD.

78: Photo by Shawn Miller, OC.

79: (top) Crosby Stuart Noyes Collection, Prints and Photographs Division, LC-DIG-jpd-00959.

79: (bottom) MMG, LCCN 2021690448.

80: (all photos) Photos by Amanda K. Reynolds, OC.

81: Photo by Shawn Miller, OC.

82: String Quartet no. 1 in D, op. 25 / Composed by Benjamin Britten / © Hawkes & Son (London) Ltd / Reproduced by permission of Boosey & Hawkes.

83: ESCFC, MD.

84: Photo by Shealah Craighead, OC.

85: (top) Inter-American Music Festivals Foundation Papers, MD.

85: (bottom) Photo by Shealah Craighead, OC.

86–88: Photos by Shawn Miller, OC.

89: (left, top and middle) Photos by Shawn Miller, OC.

89: (left, bottom) Photo by David Rice, OC.

89: (right) Photo by Shawn Miller, OC.

90: (top) Photo by Abby Brack Lewis, OC.

90: (bottom) Photo by Kevin Silverman, OC.

Act II, scene ii

91: Photo by Shawn Miller, OC.

92: Serge Koussevitzky Archive, MD.

93: MD.

94: (top) Photo by Judge Longworth, in Clara Longworth de Chambrun, *The Making of Nicholas Longworth: Annals of an American Family* (New York: Ray Long & Richard Smith, Inc., 1933), 221.

94: (bottom) and 95 (left) Photos by Shawn Miller, OC.

95: (top right) Leonora Jackson McKim Papers, MD.

96: Leonora Jackson McKim Collection, MD.

97: MMG, LCCN 2021690151

98: (left) Dina Koston and Roger Shapiro Fund for New Music, MD. Courtesy Jeffrey Mumford.

98: (right) Carolyn Royall Just Fund Collection, Music Division. Courtesy Faber Music.

99: Leonora Jackson McKim Collection, courtesy William Anderson.

100: Photo by Ruth Orkin, Irving Fine Collection, MD. Courtesy of the Ruth Orkin Archive, c/o Mary Engel.

101: Koussevitzky Music Foundation Archive, MD. Used by permission of Claudia, Emily, and Joanna Fine. (c) Hawkes & Son (London) Ltd / Reproduced by permission of Boosey & Hawkes.

102: Photo by Brandeis University. Used with permission of Brandeis University and Claudia, Emily, and Joanna Fine.

104: Courtesy of the Baltimore Symphony Orchestra.

105: (left) General Collections, MD.

105: (right) Designed by Solomon E. HaileSelassie, MD.

106–07: Photo by Shawn Miller, OC.

Act II, scene iii

108: Photo by Shawn Miller, OC.

110: (left) ESCFC, MD.

110 (right): Cartoon Drawings Collection, P&P, LC-DIG-ppmsca-10847.

111: (top) Photo by Shawn, Miller, OC.

111: (bottom) ESCFC, MD.

112: (top 3 images) Photos by Cris Alexander, courtesy of Martha Graham Resources.

112: (bottom) Courtesy of the Smithsonian National Museum of African American History and Culture and Alvin Ailey Dance Foundation, Inc., Photography by Jack Mitchell, © Alvin Ailey Dance Foundation, Inc. and Smithsonian Institution, All rights reserved.

113: Photo by Shawn Miller, OC.

114: (top) ESCFC, MD.

114: (middle) Photo by Carl Van Vechten, P&P, LC-USZ62-103962.

114: (bottom) Photo by Shawn Miller, OC.

115: (all images) MD.

116: Courtesy of the Smithsonian National Museum of African American History and Culture and Alvin Ailey Dance Foundation, Inc., Photography by Jack Mitchell, © Alvin Ailey Dance Foundation, Inc. and Smithsonian Institution, All rights reserved.

117: MMG. https://www.loc.gov/item/webcast-11277/.

118: (top and bottom) Photo by Shawn Miller, OC.

119: (top left) Photo by John T. Gibbs, OC.

119: (top right) Photo by Elaina Finkelstein, OC.

119: (bottom) Photo by Shawn Miller, OC.

120: Gershwin Collection Files, Music Division. Used with the permission of the Ira Gershwin Family.

122: (top left) P&P, LC-DIG-ppmsca-10443. Used with the permission of the George Gershwin Family and the Ira Gershwin Family.

122: (right) George and Ira Gershwin Collection, Music Division. Used with the permission of the George Gershwin Family and the Ira Gershwin Family; Music and Lyrics by GEORGE GERSHWIN and IRA GERSHWIN

© 1930 (Renewed) WC MUSIC CORP. and IRA GERSHWIN MUSIC

All Rights Administered by WC MUSIC CORP.

All Rights Reserved

Used by Permission of ALFRED MUSIC

123: Library of Congress, Prints & Photographs Division, © Nancy Lee Katz, LC-DIG-ppss-01493.

124: Photo by Elaina Finkelstein, OC.

125: Jonathan Larson Papers, MD.

126-7: Jonathan Larson Papers, Music Division.

128: (top) MMG, LCCN 2021689006.

128: (bottom) National Photo Company Collection, Prints and Photographs Division, LC-DIG-npcc-25616.

129: (top left) Photo by Shawn Miller, OC.

129: (top right) MMG, LCCN 2021689552.

129: (bottom) Photo by Allison Michael Orenstein, courtesy of the photographer.

130: (top) Photo by Elaina Finkelstein, OC.

130: (bottom) Oliver Smith Collection, MD. ©Rosaria Sinisi.

131: Tony Walton Collection, MD. Copyright © 1978 by Tony Walton.

132: Photo by Abby Brack Lewis, OC.

133: Photo by Edmond Joe, OC.

Backmatter

134: George Crumb Collection, MD. Courtesy David Crumb and Faber Music.

138, 142, 147: Photo by Shawn Miller, OC.

148: Photo of Golden String Quartet by Fernand de Gueldre. All images from ESCFC, MD.

153: GCWFC, MD.

Opposite page: Singer-songwriter Judy Collins performed in the Coolidge Auditorium on June 4, 2025. Her set included "Send in the Clowns" from *A Little Night Music* by Stephen Sondheim. Both artists' papers are held by the Music Division.

Musicians who performed at the Library often commemorated their visits with a signed publicity photo, inscribed to Coolidge and thanking her for her support.

Top left: South Mountain String Quartet, 1928.

Top right: Coolidge Quartet, undated.

Bottom left: Gordon String Quartet, 1926.

Bottom right: The English Singers, ca. 1925.

Index

Opposite page: Johannes Brahms, holograph corrections for his Symphony no. 3, op. 90, sent to publisher Robert Keller. Detail from p. 1. The Library also holds the holograph manuscript of Brahms' orchestral score of his third symphony, as well as the holograph manuscript of Brahms' arrangement of the symphony for two pianos.

(1)

Brahms' dritte Symphonie.
Correcturen u. Notizen.

I. Partitur: Hauptfehler!

p. 5: Basspos. Takt 3. d. d. (statt d. ♩♪♪) Stimme richtig.
— Viol. I. Takt 3 und 5 ist in der Stimme über dem letzten Achtel falsch! ein Punkt. Dies und manches andere auf Stricharten bezügl. ist wahrscheinlich von einem Orchesterspieler in die Stimme hineincorrigirt, welche als Vorlage f. d. Stich gedient hat.
— Violoncell. In der Stimme steht auf dem 1ten Viertel jedes Taktes ein sf. falsch!
— Contrabass / Contrafagott } Takt 3: f sf (f fehlt) besser Pag. 6

p. 6: F-Hörner sind Takt 4 anders als pag. 29.? die 1/4 Pause braucht nur einmal in der Mitte des Systems zu stehen.
Bratsche Takt 5 fehlt > über der 1ten halben Note (>)

p. 7. Clar. letzter Takt Punkt fehlt über dem 1/4 de)
Tromp. Takt 1. " " " " ersten Viertel.
Violine II. In der Stimmen heißt Takt 1 und 2 so:

Was soll gelten?

p. 8. Contrafagott Takt 3 in der Stimme steht sf unter dem 4ten a.
Viol. I. II. In den Stimmen geht der Bogen immer nur bis auf 6ten Viertel-Achtel! ?

p. 9. Takt 4 fehlt p zu Flöte II.
Bratschenstimme beide Bogen nur bis auf letzte Achtel. ?

p. 10. C-Horn II Takt 3 fehlt Taktpause.
Viol. I vorletzter Takt < zu kurz, von ersten d ab.
II " " " a
Bratsche " " " a "
Viol. II, Br. und Vcell Takt 3. 4 fehlt der Bogen wie bei Viol. I., in den Stimmen steht er jedoch.
Vcell. Takt 3 fehlt arco. Hauptfehler!
Vcell. u. CBass fehlt Takt 2 der Punkt hinter der 1/2 Pause.
Viol. I. u. II ist in der Stimme [illegible] und [illegible] gebunden? del

p. 13. Viol. I. II. in den Stimmen Takt 1: p marc.
Viol. II und Vcell: Takt 3 in den Stimmen [illegible] del
Vcell: 1tes Viertel [illegible] muss nicht gefüllt!

p. 14. 15.) Bratschenstimme: hat Schnaller: [illegible] und [illegible] del

p. 14. die Clarinetten Systeme müssten vorn in B. stehen.
Vcell Takt 3: ♯

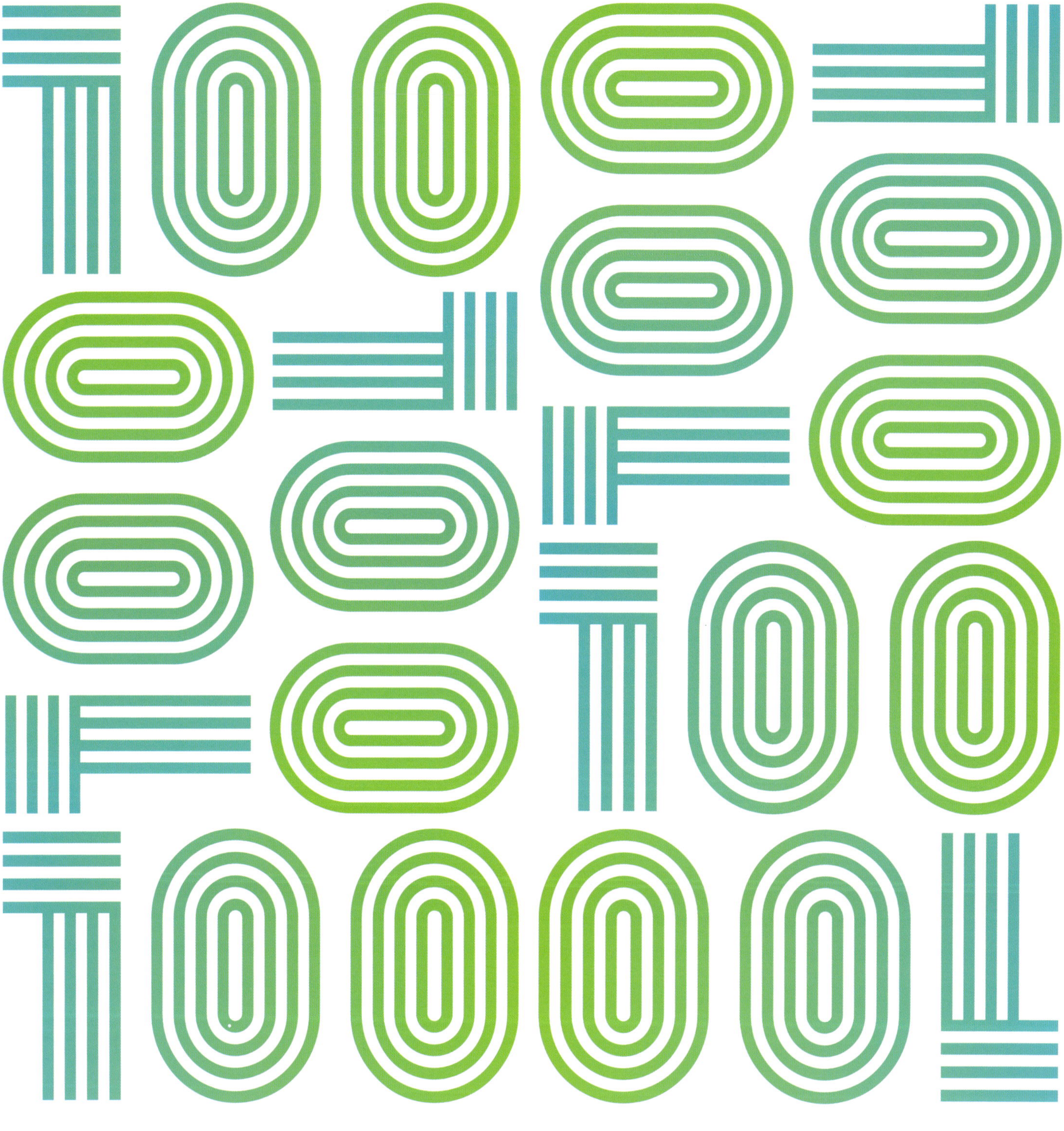